And Still Birds Sing

By the same author

Taproot
The Trespasser
Zen: Poems, Prayers, Sermons, Anecdotes, Interviews
Notes for a Guidebook
Heartland: Poets of the Midwest
World of the Buddha: An Introduction to Buddhist Literature
The Pit and Other Poems
Afterimages: Zen Poems of Shinkichi Takahashi
Twelve Death Poems of the Chinese Zen Masters
Zen Poems of China and Japan: The Crane's Bill
Awakening
Heartland II: Poets of the Midwest
Three Zen Poems
Selected Poems
Haiku of the Japanese Masters
The Duckweed Way: Haiku of Issa
The Penguin Book of Zen Poetry
The Duckpond
Prairie Voices: Poets of Illinois
Zen Poems
Encounter with Zen: Writings on Poetry and Zen
Cherries
Bird of Time: Haiku of Basho
Willows
Collected Poems 1953–1983
Traveler, My Name: Haiku of Basho
On Love and Barley: Haiku of Basho
Triumph of the Sparrow: Zen Poems of Shinkichi Takahashi
Bells of Lombardy
Of Pen and Ink and Paper Scraps
The Dumpling Field: Haiku of Issa
The Gift of Great Poetry
Cage of Fireflies: Modern Japanese Haiku
Zen, Poetry, the Art of Lucien Stryk (edited by Susan Porterfield)
The Awakened Self: Encounters with Zen
Zen Poetry: Let the Spring Breeze Enter
Where We Are: Selected Poems and Zen Translations

And Still Birds Sing

New & Collected Poems

Lucien Stryk

Swallow Press / Ohio University Press / *Athens*

Swallow Press/Ohio University Press, Athens, Ohio 45701
© 1998 Lucien Stryk
Printed in the United States of America
All rights reserved. Published 1998

Swallow Press/Ohio University Press books are printed on acid-free paper ⊗

01 00 99 98   5 4 3 2 1

"Bells of Lombardy" from *Bells of Lombardy* (1986) © Copyright 1986 by Northern Illinois
University Press. Used by permission of the publisher.

Library of Congress Cataloging-in-Publication Data
Stryk, Lucien.
    And still birds sing : new and collected poems / Lucien Stryk.
      p.   cm.
    ISBN 0-8040-1004-8 (acid-free paper). — ISBN 0-8040-1005-6 (pbk.
  : acid-free paper)
    I. Title.
PS3569.T76A82   1997
811'.54—dc21   97-27132
                                                        CIP

For Helen

Contents

From *The Pit and Other Poems* (1969)

From *Afterimages: Zen Poems of Shinkichi Takahashi* (1970)

Awakening (1973)

From *Selected Poems* (1976)

From *Collected Poems 1953–1983* (1984)

Bells of Lombardy (1986)

ONE: ROOMS

TWO: BELLS OF LOMBARDY

Of Pen and Ink and Paper Scraps (1989)

ONE: FROM THE WINDOW   223

From *Cage of Fireflies: Modern Japanese Haiku* (1993)

New Poems (1997)

Note

This collection begins with a handful of pieces, some revised, from the Fantasy Press (Oxford, England) books, *Taproot* (1953) and *The Trespasser* (1956). The poems from *Afterimages: Zen Poems of Shinkichi Takahashi* (Swallow Press, 1970) were translated with the late Takashi Ikemoto. The poems from my other Swallow Press volumes, *Notes for a Guidebook* (1965), *The Pit and Other Poems* (1969), *Awakening* (1973), *Selected Poems* (1976), *Collected Poems 1953–1983* (1984), *Of Pen and Ink and Paper Scraps* (1989), and *Cage of Fireflies: Modern Japanese Haiku* (1993), appear, mainly, in their original order. The sequence "Bells of Lombardy," from the book *Bells of Lombardy* (1986), is used with the permission of Northern Illinois University Press.

For permission to use pieces in the "New Poems" section of the book, I thank the editors and publishers of *American Poetry Review, Caprice, Collision, Haiku Quarterly, Illinois Review, New Statesman & Society, Partisan Review, Poetry Ireland Review, Printed Matter, Rafters, Seems, Tamaqua, Willow Review,* and *Contemporary American Poetry* (6th edition), edited by A. Poulin, Jr. (Houghton Mifflin, 1996).

This slowly drifting cloud is pitiful:
What dreamwalkers men become.
Awakened, I hear the one true thing—
Black rain on the roof of Fukakusa Temple.

—Dogen

From *Taproot* (1953) and *The Trespasser* (1956)

Farmer

Seasons waiting the miracle,
dawn after dawn framing
the landscape in his eyes:

bound tight as wheat, packed
hard as dirt. Made shrewd
by soil and weather, through

the channel of his bones
shift ways of animals,
their matings twist his dreams.

While night-fields quicken,
shadows slanting right, then left
across the moonlit furrows,

he shelters in the farmhouse
merged with trees, a skin of wood,
as much the earth's as his.

Southern Tale

From deep in the town the dancers' stomp
Will not rouse him now,
Where he hangs like a cracked bell:
Dark engulfs the man, the ashen cross.

The girl steps back and dreams—
O he the night and she the slippery moon,
And high the cotton flew!
It was like swimming in the river,
Water pressing to her deeps,
Ropes the arms that pulled her down,
The river banging on the wharf.

She looks away, her whiteness
Blending with the moon,
And hears the flies

Maddened by the smell of horse,
The smell of flesh.

From deep in the town the dancers' stomp
Will not rouse him now:
The arms, tongue,
Giant thighs are mute.

Mask

Behind the tattered brow
    the skull looms sharp:
as branch survives its fruits
    and wind-picked bark,
so bone releases flesh
    to weather nakedly
and lone: on winter's frost
    burns summer's day.

Scarecrow

Battered hat set firmly,
arms flapping lazily,
scarecrow's futile grimace
invites the passing crow
to feast on all the greens
a scraggy plot can grow.

Shaped by frost and sunburn,
termite and hen,
coat shreds reeking,
trousers billowing,
his windy eyes commend
beaks that snap and rend.

Long humiliation
turns him stiff and sour—

as the whole of Crowdom
from out the speckled air
feeds on rows of cabbages,
pods of plumping peas.

The Stack among the Ruins

The tangled brush and bombed-out fields reflect
And blur into the sky; harsh thunder
Rings the image to the raging sea. War
Reels again to staring eyes, where thoughts collect
In webs of fear—stirring musty brains
And hearts—then shudder through the victim veins.

No smoke lifts from the broken chimney's lip
Where winds hurl down to jar the blistered fields:
It stands alone, a maniac that yields
No breath or word, but raddled by the dip
And twist of day, turns inward to a grief
That's like an arm shaped through an empty sleeve.

There stands no more than stone on broken stone,
Yet memories converge to form a shaft of pain,—
Bruising the inner eye, scarring the brain;
Then spreading on the ruins the rusty sun
Frees the tortured mind with blasts of fire,
Flashes on the chimney stack and sags the worn barbed wire.

The Acrobat

Hands reach out to grasp the dipping rope
Which weaves an awful silence on the watching
Horde below. Taller than the crows that ring,
Their shadows shearing, through the leafless oak
The acrobat draws closer to the looping hands;
While, lifting from those fatal arms, his eye
Seeks images that swarm across the sky,
Then fall through boughs to merge with twisting strands.

The air grows tense within the bracing bow of day.
The hands are raised to snap the dancing cord.

Words that sought his tongue remain unsaid—
Torn in his throat. Above, the branches sway
Against the wind's astonished flank. The horde
Draws back from where his hugeness dangles dead.

Chu Ming-How

Chu Ming-How, the Mandarin,
Astride his fat brown mule,
Rode slowly up a high green hill
To dodge the lowland din,
  The tassel on the mule's long tail
  Swished gaily in the sun.

Half-way up the mule sat down
And drowsy Chu fell back,
Removed his shoes and dusty pack
And dozed upon the ground,
  The scarlet button on his cloak
  Cast scarlet all around.

But still into his wise old head
The lowland troubles crept
So on the mule's moist rump he leapt
And flogged his way ahead,
  The cherries on the hill were grouped
  In patterns white and red.

Then under a dripping cherry tree
He unrolled his silk and pen
And while the mule brayed down the sun
He sketched the rose-blue sky,
  Which wore a tasseled button
  Above the shading tree.

Notes for a Guidebook (1965)

The Beachcomber

Beyond the patchwork bobbing of her back
The nineteen peaks of Sado float
In violet mist. Below, the "Exiles' Route"
Is taut with sail and net. Across
The humps of sand that blot the sea
The pinetrees hold the beaten shore,
And just as she is wasted by a cold
Necessity, the iced Siberian wind
Has bent and shriveled to their salty core.

She dreams a raft of treasure to her reach:
A silky foam will wash ten lacquered bowls
Like frozen blossoms to the beach,
And she will pluck them with a girlish hand.
Now as the sunset, like a vulgar fan,
Spreads slowly on the exiled peaks
She scoops and hurls a pebble at the waves.
But nothing happens. From those crystal founts
The frail and scattered richness never breaks.

Hearn in Matsue

That all was miniature gave him comfort
    Of a sort,
And after the Lady, Ellen Freeman,

To whom he had written finally, "Do not
    Disgust me,
Please—" the women were so otherworldly

It was like a permanent exhibition
    For which one
Scarcely had to be the connoisseur. In fact

He shut his eyes and took the nearest for both
    Bed and name
(He had tired of his); was bowed into a house

Which brushed the river a crane's cry from the
    Daimyo's Tower;
Started fussing with the garden; pushed his wife's

Few things around the room like chessmen; until,
    Pleased at last,
He braced for winter which, though wet, was very

Beautifying. He was often seen tramping from
    The bathhouse,
Flesh a-tingle, all rose against the snow.

Came time to work: a cub again, he snuffed for
    News in Old
Japan, and, stiff on haunches, englished along

With a nameless one or two, tales which drew
    The expert's
Touch like lacquered puzzle-boxes and, when solved,

Would gush from prospects charged with mountains
    Called Giraffes,
Trees tense as wire, a moon which always snared

In pineboughs, and temples which could pull one
    To the knees.
The fame did not surprise: it had awaited

Him like those fragrant ports of forty
    Years ago
The tall black hulls of home. It fit him, and he

Wore it as he felt, deservingly. What as
    Years crept by
He would not learn to bear, and ill deserved,

Was wife, friends, job, food, the too familiar
    Land itself,
And now, in winter, the Siberian wind

That tore across the sea to heap him at
    The brazier
For months, weak eyes pricked by dying charcoal.

It was then, remembering Shelley and his
    Fading coal,
He knew how much he hated all Romance.

Return to Hiroshima

I. Bombardier

Coming out of the station he expected
To bump into the cripple who had clomped,
Bright pencils trailing, across his dreams

For fifteen years. Before setting out
He was ready to offer both his legs,
His arms, his sleepless eyes. But it seemed

There was no need: it looked a healthy town,
The people gay, the new streets dancing
In the famous light. Even the War Museum

With its photos of the blast, the well-mapped
Rubble, the strips of blackened skin,
Moved one momentarily. After all,

From the window one could watch picnickers
Plying chopsticks as before, the children
Bombing carp with rice-balls. Finding not

What he had feared, he went home cured at last.
Yet minutes after getting back in bed
A wood leg started clomping, a thousand

Eyes leapt wild, and once again he hurtled
Down a road paved white with flesh. On waking
He knew he had gone too late to the wrong

Town, and that until his own legs numbed
And eyes went dim with age, somewhere
A fire would burn that no slow tears could quench.

II. Pilot

All right, let them play with it,
Let them feel all hot and righteous,
Permit them the savage joy of

Deploring my inhumanity,
And above all let them bury
Those hundred thousands once again:

I too have counted the corpses,

And say this: if Captain X
Has been martyred by the poets,
Does that mean I have to weep

Over his "moments of madness"?
If he dropped the bomb, and he did,
If I should sympathize, and I do

(I too have counted the corpses),

Has anyone created a plaint
For those who shot from that red sun
Of Nineteen Forty-One? Or

Tried to rouse just one of those
Thousand Jonahs sprawled across
The iron-whale bed of Saipan Bay?

I too have counted the corpses.

And you, Tom Staines, who got it
Huddled in "Sweet Lucy" at my side,
I still count yours, regretting

You did not last to taste the
Exultation of learning that
"Perhaps nine out of ten of us"

(I too have counted the corpses)

Would not end up as fertilizer
For next spring's rice crop. I'm no
Schoolboy, but give me a pencil

And a battlefield, and I'll make you
A formula: take one away
From one, and you've got bloody nothing.

I too have counted the corpses.

III. Survivors

Of the survivors there was only one
That spoke, but he spoke as if whatever
Life there was hung on his telling all.

And he told all. Of the three who stayed,
Hands gripped like children in a ring, eyes
Floating in the space his wall had filled,

Of the three who stayed on till the end,
One leapt from the only rooftop that
Remained, the second stands gibbering

At a phantom wall, and it's feared the last,
The writer who had taken notes, will
Never write another word. He told all.

The Mine: Yamaguchi

It is not hell one thinks of, however dark,
These look more weary than tormented.
One would expect, down there, a smell more human,
A noise more agonized than that raised
By cars shunted, emptied, brimmed again.

Today, remembering, the black heaps themselves
(On which conveyors drop, chip by chip,
What aeons vised and morselled to lay
A straw of light across the page)
Do not force infernal images.

After weeks of trying to forget,
The eye resists, the vision begged and gotten

Is the heart's: rows of women bent over
Feed-belts circling like blood, pickhammers
Biting at the clods that trundle by,

Raw hands flinging waste through scuttles gaped behind
While, a stone's-throw down the company road,
A smokestack grits the air with substance one
Might sniff below, or anywhere. It marks
The crematory, they pass it twice a day.

The Revolutionary

Who was it said that men to forge beyond
Must jell into a mob composed of as
Many minds, fused singly, as it has heads?

A monster-maker with a taste for blood,
He would have lumped the lot and had us
Leaping impassables, breaching impregnables.

Four hundred years before the birth of Christ,
Mencius, advisor to the King of Ch'i,
Saw man as such, and in a scarlet notebook

Laid at his liege's feet, had planted characters
So rich of seed, so thick with hate of all
That eye surveyed, the tribe of lackey scholars

Gathered by the princes to find fault,
Each weighted with a royal scythe and bearing,
In wormy fist, the straw of abuse all life's-blood

Had been spent for, fell panting across the sage's tomb.
The Chinese are a thorough, hardy race,
But the Court was overstocked with geldings,

And who, however formidable,
Could have held back those squat black ships,
Crammed to the sails with early-harvest grain,

From plying westward, port to hungry port?

Moharram

(Islam: month of mourning)

Where we ate in the canyon
The stream reflected, on the crags,
A hundred wavering heads
And the sun falling laced
The water with their blood.
When the sheep grazed down
To clatter round our fire
They wore those heads again,
And the stream had cleansed
The blood from every throat.

Yet none could feel at ease
As, catching our breath, we watched
The shepherd yelp them past
Gorged with the darkened grass.
By that afternoon of Tassua,
Stretched in a great arc of thirst,
The mourners of Hoseyn had flecked
The cragstones with their salt—
Tears, gigantic, rolled down to swell
The trickle misnamed stream.

The water was unfit to drink
And it burned the fingers where
The spits had turned in unbelievers'
Hands. When the sun went down
The sheep, dragging their puffy
Dugs, cropped past again to fold.
Tomorrow was Ashura, day
Of human sacrifice, not sheep's,
And blood would spatter round the gate
Of Imam Reza's Shrine.

Though safely distant, already
We could hear from the city fading
At our backs the cry of "Ya Hoseyn!"
And as on a thousand tambours
Borne as one the rough palms of mourners
Slapped against stripped chests. We bound

The spits, still smelling of our feast,
With wire, and leaving the canyon
To the dark, filed slowly down
The path those jaws had cleared.

The Woman Who Lived in a Crate

She was very famous: three times she'd sailed
    The world around
In books of photographs, pressed against the
    Imam Reza's Shrine.

Summers she would squat inside the crate,
    Cracked almsbowl up,
Ten *rials* a snapshot, jaw clenched miserably
    For an extra five.

Then as the tourist scuttled off, out poked
    Veiled head, and she
Would crawl onto the sodden road to
    Spit the money clean

And gossip with the roadsweep's mule. Guiltily
    We bore her scraps
Until we saw it was ourselves, trapped in
    Thick-walled crate, we might

Have pitied: no-one picked shamed way through
    Steaming mule-turds
To fill a leaky almsbowl, while we sat
    Tittering in the sun.

A Pipe of Opium

When I dropped to the floor
And Jahangir my friend,
Squatting above me, stuffed

The pellets in and lit them,
Enjoining me to puff,
His family started giggling.

At first euphoria of sorts,
Then a quick dissolving: Jahangir
And all his portly brood

Became an undertaker, seven-voiced,
Many fingered, and for an age
I stalked the purgatory

Of his atrocious living room,
Watching the Kerman carpet's
Garden wilt around me,

Feeling the Farsi cackle
Boom against the skull. I rose
Headachy and wiser. There are

Many ways to dodge reality,
Hundreds of states preferable
To the kind of life we own,

But the only satisfactory death
Takes us clean-lunged, clear-headed,
And very much alone.

A Persian Suite

I. Delgusha Garden

The bulbuls do not sing here
    Anymore,
And the streambeds, dammed with silt,

Do not rise to lap the
    Scented toes
Of lovers dawdling under

Aspens with Khayyam. Am I
    Alone in
Liking it this way? It was

All too much, too much, smelling
    Of Genghis
Khan and Tamerlane. Whoever

Flung those gates apart and shoved
    A horde of
Muddy beggars through to foul

The footpaths, dip sour rags
    Into the
Pond, deserves our thanks. Now

The pond's an ossuary.
    The beggars
Do not come here anymore.

And rocking the aspens, hid
    By leaves, crows
Rain droppings, and fly on.

II. Beggars

Like distressed ships they founder
    In ocean
That has never ceased to batter,

However calm the instruments
      Pronounce it,
Their arms like broken spars

Stretched for the saving pittance.
      Though the day
Be windless their rags blow wild,

And oh their mouths send out such
      Piteous
Signals, forever more the food

Must turn to garbage on the
      Painted dish.
They cry, but the fog is thick

And full of plunging monsters
      And the firm
Ships sailing by cannot shift

A sole degree from a course
      As rigid
As the Table of the Laws,

Those bent coins boiling in the wake
      Would scarcely
Fill the stomach of a gull.

III. Oasis

Nothing stands so green.
These few trees hold back
      A tide of sand

And ride the grit-blast,
Or moving with the sun,
      Which all day long

Nibbles at the grass-edge,
Twist like dervishes in
      The pool below.

Imam Reza, from all
Sides your pilgrim trails
    Stretch parched as tongues,

And chanting your name,
Balanced between water
    And death, they come.

IV. The Dome

All gold, the pilgrims heap
Like coals beneath your
    Radiance.

Forever set, the wheeling
Sun must envy you. How
    Bright you burn!

Only the prophet, brooding
In the dark, knows you for
    What you are:

Bauble of Allah, how
Many sinners have purchased
    Peace with you?

V. Desert Song

Shall we strike the tent now,
    And move on
Beneath the terrible sun?

We are searchers together,
    You and I,
For that the world thinks madness.

Well, let them call it so!
    What can they
Know, those bitter ones who

Wallow on the seven shores,
        Of the sweet
Rush of water to the

Aching throat? Or how dream
        The wonder
Of need beyond fulfillment?

Enough! Again I have found
        Oasis
In the cool streams of your arms.

VI. *Muezzin*

It is a matter no longer of finding
        The most durable voice:
There are records of the best, and loudspeakers

Perch like parrots in the muezzin's cage
        Atop the minaret.
So one is not greatly stirred, being

American and here for only a year,
        By all the business
Around the Imam Reza's Shrine. Yet

Walking absurdly about at always
        Brilliant noon, one can be
Hurled to the shadows when, mincing past

The beggars at the gate, black from top
        To toe, veil bulged bonily
Over nose, eyes which see but cannot,

By God, be seen plunged to the unclean heart,
        Comes woman to her prayer.
Then let all those parrots croak together,

One's still in Persia, a thousand years ago.

A Sheaf for Chicago

Something queer and terrifying about Chicago: one of the strange "centres" of the earth ...
—D. H. Lawrence to Harriet Monroe

I. Proem

Always when we speak of you, we call you
Human. You are not. Nor are you any
Of the things we say: queer, terrifying.

It is the tightness of the mind that would
Confine you. No more strange than Paris
Is gay, you exist by your own laws,

Which to the millions that call you theirs,
Suffice, serve the old gargantuan needs.
Heaped as if just risen—streaming, unsmirched—

From seethings far below, you accept all.
By land, air, sea they come, certain to find
You home. For those you've once possessed, there's no

Escaping: always revealed in small
Particulars—a bar, a corner—you
Reappear complete. Even as I address

You, seeing your vastness in alleyways
And lots that fester Woodlawn, I have
A sense of islands all around, made one

By sea—that feeds and spoils yet is a thing
Apart. You are that sea. And home: have
Stamped me yours for keeps, will claim me when,

Last chances spent, I wrap it up for good.
You are three million things, and each is true.
But always home. More so and more deeply

Than the sum of antheaps we have made of
You, reenter every night to dream you
Something stone can never be. And met

However far away, two that call you
Home, feel beyond the reach of words to tell
Like brothers who must never part again.

II. A Child in the City

In a vacant lot behind a body shop
I rooted for your heart, O city,
The truth that was a hambone in your slop.

Your revelations came as thick as bees,
With stings as smarting, wings as loud,
And I recall those towering summer days

We gathered fenders, axles, blasted hoods
To build Cockaigne and Never-never Land,
Then beat for dragons in the oily weeds.

That cindered lot and twisted auto mound,
That realm to be defended with the blood,
Became, as New Year swung around,

A scene of holocaust, where pile on pile
Of Christmas trees would char the heavens
And robe us demon-wild and genie-tall

To swirl the hell of 63rd Place,
Our curses whirring by your roofs,
Our hooves a-clatter on your face.

III. The Balloon

(To Auguste Piccard, his day at Soldier Field)

As you readied the balloon, tugging
At the ropes, I grabbed my father's hand.
Around us in stone tiers the others

Began to hold their breath. I watched my
Father mostly, thinking him very
Brave for toying with his pipe. Then when

You filled the giant sack with heated
Air and, waving, climbed into the
Gondola with a bunch of roses

Thrust at you, I freed my hand, cheered
And started clapping. I caught your eye,
You smiled, then left the ground. The people

Filed for exits when, twisting in
The wind, you veered above the lake, a
Pin against a thundercloud. But I

Refused to budge. My father stooped to
Beat me and cracked his precious briar
On the stone. And still I wouldn't leave.

He called me a young fool and dragged me,
Bawling, to the streetcar. But I couldn't
Stop watching you. I stayed up all that night,

Soaring ever higher on your star,
Through tunneled clouds and air so blue
I saw blue spots for hours. In the morning

My father laughed and said you came back down.
I didn't believe him then, and never will.
I told him I was glad he broke his pipe.

IV. The Beach

Even the lake repulses:
I watch them where, shellacked
      And steaming

In barbaric light, they
Huddle in their shame, the maids
      And busboys.

Even the lovers dare not
Step where the goddess rose in
      Tinted foam,

But paw each other, gape,
Spin radio dials. And hulking
    Over cards

Mothers whip strings of
Curse like lariats, jerking
    The children

From the shore when, suddenly
Across the beach, they hear:
    "Lost! Child lost!"

None rise. The breakers drown
Voices, radios; peak white, pound
    In like fists.

V. Mestrovic's Indians

(Equestrian statues, Michigan Avenue)

With bare heels sharp as spurs
They kick the bronze flanks of
    The horses.

But what sane beast would brave
A river wild as this, choked
    As it is

With jagged tin and all
That snarling rubber? and
    Ford to where?

Along the other bank, while the
Great arms pointing with their
    Manes convulse

In anger, the merchants
Dangle strings of gewgaws
    In the sun.

But no mere hoof was meant
For plunging here, and why, the
    Horses seem

To ask, would even redskins
Climb a shore where not one
    Grassblade springs?

VI. *City of the Wind*

All night long the lake-blast
    Rattled bones of
Dreamers in that place of glass.

Awake, they heard a roaring
    Down the lots and
Alleyways where wind flung

Rainspout, fencepost, toolshed,
    As if the town
Were tossing on the flood

Of space. All night, it seemed,
    A horde of giants
Came trampling overhead,

Tore limbs, wrenched screens, spilled
    Glass like chips of
Sky. Next day through, the dazed

Ones rooted in the mire,
    Then, back in beds,
Dreamt the city fairer

Than before. But how,
    Snapped antennae
Pulling roofs askew,

Autos tipped hub-deep in silt,
    Could dream raise up
What dream alone had built?

VII. *Eve*

In Calcutta I found her in a stall,
    A thing for sale,
Breasts like burnished gourds: some things one does not buy.

In Isfahan her eyes were black as wells
    Entreating alms
Of all who passed: there are deserving charities.

    In Amsterdam above a darkened street
        A bay window
Framed her sundries, proffering bliss: I was not sold.

    In Seville she wore a gypsy shawl and
        Bangles on her
Dancing feet: the silver dropped around them was not mine.

    In Paris she hugged me down the avenue,
        Skirt a jocund
Sail, towed by the dollars in my purse: I tacked for home.

    In Chicago she waits behind a door
        No common key
Can budge: who enters there will never get away.

VIII. The Gang

One can hardly extricate them
From the props they lounge against,
Or see them for the smoke lips

Link in chains that will not hold.
At night the sound of pennies tossed
Upon the sidewalk-cracks is like

A slowly breaking mirror
Which reflects the little that they
Are. What girl dare pass and not

Be whistled at? Their appraisements
Are quick, absolute: that water
Freezes into ice needs scant

Deliberation. Whatever
The day sweeps up, their sole
Antagonist is boredom, which

By merely standing around, they
Thwart at every turn but one.
They scorn whom others envy,

The man who ambles by, duty
Snapping at the heels, and should lovers
Cross, there is a sudden flinging down

(By eyes so starved, they almost moan)
And then a coupling in the dust.
Allow them such years to lean

And wait. Soon they must approach
The selfsame corner, and hail
The gang that is no longer there.

IX. *The Neighborhood*

Long away, I find it pure
Exotic; no matter that they roll
The sidewalks up at ten and boys

Want height to leap for basketballs:
It is a place, and there are corners
Where one does what one would do.

Come back, I find the expected
Changes: shabby streets grown shabbier,
The mob all scattered, old girl friends

Losing more of what's been lost,
The supermarts turned up like sows
To give the brood of grunters suck,

And Mother, like a thickening tree
Whose roots work deeper as the woodsman
Nears, spread over all, the wind which sweeps

Across her whispering "Stay on."
Two weeks of that, and there are
Other whispers that I heed.

The train pulls in and I descend,
To mount before it pulls away.
Goodby, Mother, goodby! I'm off

Again to Someplace Else, where
Chafing together once a month
The strangers sit and write sweet letters home.

Notes for a Guidebook

In celestial Padua
The ghosts walk hugely
In the public squares.

Donatello is one,
His horseman in the
Piazza San Antonio
Guards the gruff saint's heart
Like a mystic ruby,
The ears of the horse,
Of the rider,
Riddled by prayer.

Giotto, Dante are others,
The painter's frescoes
Float like clouds
Above the city,
The poet's cantos
Ring upon its walls.

And what of us,
Who stand with heads
Strained back, feet tapping?
Shall we eat, sleep,
Be men again?
Shall we slip back
To the whores of Venice?—
Dwarfs, clods, motes of dust
In the brightness.

The Fountain of Ammanati

(Piazza della Signoria, Florence)

Below the pigeon-spotted seagod
The mermen pinch the mermaids,
And you shopgirls eat your food.

No sneak-vialed aphrodisiac
Can do—for me, for you—what
Mermen pinching mermaids in a whack

Of sunlit water can. And do.
These water-eaten shoulders and these thighs
Shall glisten though your gills go blue.

These bones will never clatter in the breath.
My dears, before your dust swirls either up
Or down—confess: this world is richly wet.

And consider: there is a plashless world
Outside this stream-bright square
Where girls like you lie curled

And languishing for love like mine.
And you were such as they
Until ten sputtering jets began

To run their ticklish waters down your
Spine. Munch on, my loves, you are but
Sun-bleached maidens in a world too poor

To tap the heart-wells that would flow,
And flow. You are true signorine
Of that square where none can go

And then return. Where dusty mermen
Parch across a strand of sails and spars,
And dream of foamy thighs that churn.

Torero

Some see him dancer,
Delight as the banderillas
Hit and quiver from his practiced hand,
Fall like a savage
Bird, piece by piece, talons piercing.
Yet there are those
Who cheer him as compassionate butcher,
Sniff the wild flesh on the hospital table,
Marvel as sharp ribs expand, hunger
Fades from the eyes of widows and orphans.

Others see him priest,
Pray as he sights along the sword,
Hosanna as he plunges toward the altar,
See the swordhilt as
Chalice spilling hot as flame, take the host
Of the ears, the tail,
While he circles the arena
And is pelted by hats, fans, a hundred
Twisted flowers. As the dead bull
Is dragged along the sand, these cross themselves.

And there are some
Who see great panniers choked
With easy pesetas, their gambler hearts
Choking with love
As he kneels before the bull, spreads glistering arms:
Only the torero,
Sad face stiff with fear, sees the bull.
Beyond the shrines in cheap hotels, the heaped pesetas,
The villa by the sea—horns
Like a fist of knives brush him in the dark.

In a Spanish Garden

Aranjuez, he remembered waking—
Jardin de la Isla. He lay
All night among the trampled roses
And high above him now
The one-armed faun, features haggard
In the dewy light, stared down
Like a conqueror. Somewhere
At his back a fountain dripped.

He sat up dazed and, groping round,
Snatched and shook the bottle
Like a club. The goatboy did not budge,
The fountain kept on dripping,
The scent of roses was as sour
As puke. And as he moved up
To the hedge, those little mouths
Were snapping at his heels.

Straddling the hedge, he whooped and toppled
Headlong to the path when, popping
From a lilac bush, he saw a pitchfork
Then a beard. Such screams pierced
All around him, the very leaves
Screwed up to buds again. And then
It was he heard the pounding of
A thousand hoofs upon wet gravel.

He scrambled up the ornamental gate
And, rocking there, watched until
He thought him blind the pitchforks flashing
At his feet like waves. He whooped again
And kicked his heels into the bars
Like bronco ribs. And then he cried—
Your bloody roses! *Caramba!*
If this is Eden, where the hell is God?

The Road from Delphi

The twin prophetic streams still running through
Our heads, we drank above the gorge and watched
The eagles. You remembered, as sunset
Forged a halo over you and stained
The clear wine red, the country's tragedy.
Too much history, I said, erodes the best of lands.

Yet passing Thebes again, this time in darkness,
You spoke of Oedipus, his darkness,
And now the rattling of the bus became
The work of furies. I smiled knowingly
But envied the cunning of your sex
Which makes of the flintiest peak a roost in time.

Escale

One remembers a port where boats
    Tap fitfully
Against wharf-poles and wharf-side shops,

Patched awnings taut, are cool as
    Sunlit fathoms.
At times the rooftops of the town

Swim like brilliant shoals the washed
    And briny air.
One remembers a bar where fish-soup's

On all hours and sailors wait the
    Windfall virgins
Of long sea-rocked nights. There, on a

Shimmered terrace, steeped in acrid
    Afternoons, they
Lean across the tables, burning,

To watch years slip like freighters
       Down the seaways.
And there remain, knowing the worst

Of inland days, the rot, the sloth,
       The ennui, to
Tramp in dream the unmarked shore.

Chekhov in Nice

I

Along the Boulevard des Anglais
Tourists mistook him for Lautrec,
Though he was taller
And when not hunched over hacking
His walk was straight enough.

Perhaps it was the way he stared
At women, like a beggar
At a banquet window, and then
He was always scrabbling for a notebook
While the snickering revelers

Flowed like water round a stone.
Oh they all knew him artist.
All, that is, except the people
He would talk to in his
Scant atrocious French: the waiter,

The cabdriver, the man who
Brought his boots back in the morning
Like an oblation to Apollo.
To them he was a munificent
White Russian, title snatched,

A parcel of serfs languishing
For his return. Certainly
He was unhappy. And the chambermaids

Were touched by nailmarks
Through the blood-flecks on his sheet.

The century had just turned over,
And the Côte was never gayer.
Even the dowagers, strapped
To beachchairs all along the shore,
Felt young again and very beautiful.

And rather scornful, he was quick
To see, of the old-young man
Who moved among them like a noctambule,
His back to Mother Russia,
Seagulls screaming at his ears.

II

He had just turned forty, and now
At times he felt himself regretting.
Oh they had expected far too much
Of one as sick and poor, hung with
Unmarried sisters and a widowed dam.

Wasn't it enough to have planted
The usual imaginary garden?
Must he also, like some poet,
Sing upon the ruddy boughs?
Were he less the son, he'd have come

Here twenty years ago. Before those
Germs, swarming, had carved
A kingdom of his chest, before
The flame had risen from his bowels
To fan within his head. Were he less the son. . . .

And the reputation, so harshly won,
Did precious little good in France.
Who'd risk displeasing one who'd make of her,
However high her beauty,
A thing of pity in some dismal tale?

Foutu! he muttered as he slunk
Back to his room and tossed his hat

Upon the pile of doodled papers
On the desk. Now he longed for home.
In the few years left to him

Would come—was bound to come—
Another thirty stories and a dozen plays.
Then no doubt they'd prop his bones
Between those giants in Novo-Devechy.
But were there any choice to make, he'd act

The part of one the world was still applauding,
That country squire of his,
Petulant, bored, pining for the Côte d'Azur,
And—if one could believe those Russian hacks—
Likely to live forever.

Words on a Windy Day

Airing out the clothes,
        The odor of mothballs
                Driving me inside,
I watch in wonder
        As the wind fills
                Trouserlegs and sweaters,

Whips them light and dark.
        In that frayed coat
                I courted her a year,
In that old jacket
        Married her, then brushed
                Her tears off with a sleeve.

The wind blows through them,
        Tosses them about,
                These mildewed ghosts of love
That life, for lack of something
        Simple as a clothespin,
                Let fall, one by one.

The Rock

Year after year he returned to the same
Spot, hoping for a change. But found
No change, except that sometimes
The water was darker, sometimes
The beach was littered, sometimes not.

Month after month he thought as he
Imagined the journey back,
This time all will be different,
This time the rock will stand free,
Pushed back the shrouding sea.

But always, except that sometimes
The water tossed darker, sometimes
As light as cloud, the sea
Would reach the place on the rock
His head had dashed with blood.

And this distressed him. For
If the sea was changeless,
Except for the color, except for
The look of the beach, he was not.
As he saw when bent across

The rock, his face a scum upon
The moving water. Yet year
After year he came back to look again,
Until the bloodstain on the rock
Was like a sleeping eye, washed

By the hissing foam, until they had
To hold him as he scraped across
The sand. Dropping their pails
Below the rock like explorers
Come to the one and only place.

And made a castle there beside
The rock. Year after year
The grandchildren returned, and saw
The water lapping on the rock,
And thought of him, and thought of death.

From *The Pit and Other Poems* (1969)

Oeuvre

Will it ever be finished, this house
  Of paper
I began to raise when I was seventeen?

Others scramble from foundations far less firm.
  Seasons of
Pondering, name by name, the past's magnificent,

A squandering. Surely I might have lived.
  Spitefully
Watching as rivals stole the girls, got the jobs,

Won the laurels, the misery seeped in,
  Tinting the
Windows, darkening the fairest day.

But how should I have known, a house to please
  Need not be
Outlandish? And that searching everywhere

The fresh, the rare, prowling the gaudier
  Capitals,
Something of each would rub off, deface.

Well, we build where and as we can. There are
  Days when I
Am troubled by an image of the house,

Laden, rootless, like a tinseled tree,
  Suddenly
Torn to a thousand scribbled leaves and borne off

By the wind, then to be gathered and patched
  Whole again,
Or of the thing going up in smoke

And I, the paper dreamer, wide awake.

To a Japanese Poet

You stood frozen there,
One hand gripping my arm,
In the other your lunchbasket,
And when I turned
To look into your face,
It was like witnessing a birth.

When the poem came,
Your fingers loosened and you
Spoke the dozen words as if
Directing one who'd
Lost his way upon
A mountain path, the night descending.

Finally we went to join
The others, but you were not the same.
All that brilliant autumn day
You avoided me
As if I'd surprised you
In some intimacy, as if my being

Near had suddenly
Cut us off. Later, when I mentioned
A hurt no memory of scarlet leaves
Could ease, you laughed
And said, "Why should you
Have felt badly? We had an enjoyable outing."

Zen: The Rocks of Sesshu

(Joei Temple Garden, Yamaguchi)

I

What do they think of
   Where they lean
Like ponderous heads, the rocks?—

In prankish spring, ducks
   Joggling here
And there, brushing tails,

Like silly thoughts shared,
   Passed from head
To head? When, gong quavering

About a ripened sky, we
   Up and go,
Do they waken from a dream of flesh?

II

In the Three Whites of
   Hokusai—
Fuji, the snow, the crane—

What startles is the black: in
   The outline
Of the mountain, the branch-tips

Piercing the snow, the quills of
   The crane's wing:
Meaning impermanence.

Here, in stainless air, the
   Artist's name
Blazes like a crow.

III

Distance between the rocks,
    Half the day
In shadow, is the distance

Between man who thinks
    And the man
Who thinks he thinks: wait.

Like a brain, the garden,
    Thinking when
It is thought. Otherwise

A stony jumble, merely that,
    Laid down there
To stud our emptiness.

IV

Who calls her butterfly
    Would elsewhere
Pardon the snake its fangs:

In the stony garden
    Where she flits
Are sides so sharp, merely

To look gives pain. Only
    The tourist,
Kodak aimed and ready for

The blast, ship pointing for the
    Getaway,
Dare raise that parasol.

V

To rid the grass of weed, to get
    The whole root,
Thick, tangled, takes a strong mind

And desire—to make clean, make pure.
   The weed, tough
As the rock it leaps against,

Unless plucked to the last
   Live fiber
Will plunge up through dark again.

The weed also has the desire
   To make clean,
Make pure, there against the rock.

VI

It is joy that lifts those pigeons to
   Stitch the clouds
With circling, light flashing from underwings.

Scorning our crumbs, tossed carefully
   To corners
Of the garden, beyond the rocks,

They rose as if summoned from
   The futile
Groveling our love subjects them to.

Clear the mind! Empty it of all that
   Fixes you,
Makes every act a pecking at the crumb.

VII

Firmness is all: that mountain beyond the
   Garden path,
Watch how against its tawny slope

The candled boughs expire. Follow
   The slope where
Spearheads shake against the clouds

And dizzy the pigeons circling on the wind.
    Then observe
Where no bigger than a cragstone

The climber pulls himself aloft,
    As by the
Very guts: firmness is all.

VIII

Pierced through by birdsong, stone by stone
    The garden
Gathered light. Darkness, hauled by ropes

Of sun, entered roof and bough. Raised from
    The temple
Floor where, stiff since cockcrow,

Blown round like Buddha on the lotus,
    He began
To write. How against that shimmering,

On paper frail as dawn, make poems?
    Firm again,
He waited for the rocks to split.

The Quake

Alone in that paper house
We laughed when the bed
Heaved twice then threw
Us to the floor. When all

Was calm again, you said
It took an earthquake
To untwine us. Then I
Stopped your shaking

With my mouth. Together
In this place of brick,
Held firm as fruits
Upon a sculptured bough,

Our loving is more safe.
Then why should dream
Return us to that fragile
Shelf of land? And why,

Our bodies twined upon
This couch of stone,
Should we be listening,
Like dead sinners, for the quake?

H. S. with Noh Mask

Unpacking again, tired, fearing
    Another drought,
You plunge an arm into the trunk

And, holding the mask against your
    Face, stand before
The mirror searching the self

I made you leave behind: dark hair
    Flowing with its
Three loose strands, eyes burning back

To where you always are, cheeks
    Like sides of tusks
And there, through parted lips

The squares of blackened teeth which
    Alone are strange.
How naturally you pose in time

Back here in Chicago
    Where tomorrow,
Noh mask hung upon the wall,

You must try to make a life.

Return to DeKalb

Expecting no miracle, we found none:
One retarred blacktop, another supermart,
    The sum of change—

Apart from the waiting neighbors, in which
Plentiful loss of hair and swollen girth,
    Those additions

To a catalogue of woes, came as small
Surprise. We were the lucky travelers
    Come back to plan

A further flight, happy to learn that none
Remembered an earthquake in Persia or
    Rioting in Greece.

Suddenly sick of so much reality,
We climbed the long-worn staircase to the
    Bedroom, and found

What each had thought was shaken off—Time
Rose stinking from the mattress, perched, a
    Raven, on the sill.

The Anniversary

The sun rising,
  The sun setting,
Takes no more beauty
  On than yours
Whom the years have
  Carried like a vessel
Across the grinding seas.

I ride you like
  A Sinbad, seeking
What I have but
  Cannot find until
The Roc lies plucked
  And bleeding on
The shore all sailors curse.

O love, this ten years'
  Voyage in your arms
Has taught me nothing
  That I did not know
When, sighting you, I swam
  To board the one fair ship
Among the blistered prows.

Voyager

And how he pities the man with an arm
About the girl who, like a tug, guides
Him through the high sea of aloneness,
Certain to toss him on the nearest shore,

Should another beckon. Forever solitary,
How he feels for those that go, two by two,
In the illusion of togetherness.
Watching outside the Greyhound Station

For the carriage that will take him anywhere,
He is part of all: in every city
Painted mouths are pouting to be bruised,
A thousand sheets, stretching like a snowfield,

Await the restless imprint of his limbs.
The voyager can cherish the heart fulfilled
For its illusion of fulfillment
As he moves in the dream of arrival.

Lover

Always the exile
Learning a strange landscape,
    Unsure

Of self, certain only
Of the moon, despite her
    New face

And the memory,
Vaguely troubling as
    Her light,

Of promises in
A country true
    As this.

Étude

I was cycling by the river, back and forth,
    Umbrella up against the
        Rain and blossoms.

It was very quiet, I thought of Woolworth
    Globes you shake up snowstorms in.
        Washed light slanted

Through the cherry trees, and in a flimsy house
    Some youngster practiced Chopin.
        I was moving

With the current, wheels squishing as the music
    Rose into the trees, then stopped,
        And from the house

Came someone wearing too much powder, raincape
    Orchid in the light. Middle-aged,
        The sort you pass

In hundreds everyday and scarcely notice,
    The Chopin she had sent
        Up to those boughs,

Petals spinning free, gave her grace no waters
    Would reflect, but I might
        Long remember.

That Woman There

Will she ever go away, that woman there?
Every night she stands with arms upraised,
High throat twisting in the streetlamp's noose.

One by one they come, the wild beseechers—
Merchants, students, thieves, he who squats before,
Shaking a bouquet of dollars at her knees.

O she is cruel to keep them, eyes plucking
At these half-drawn blinds. What does she hope
To offer, fingers spread, sharp heels grinding?

Must she be told that He has left for good?

Song for One

After the wedding,
The flung rice and boots,
   The guests like fountains
Gushing on the lawn
    (Her arms around him
    Like a noose)
It was good to get out of town,
   Lay her down
  In the dark of a room
He would never see again.

After the honeymoon,
Niagara and the Empire State,
   The coins and tokens
Pelting from his purse
    (Her body like a doe
    Lashed to a hood)
It was sad to get back to town,
   Lay her down
  In the dark of a room
He had hated from the start.

The Locusts

Whirring from the desert, so dense
   We thought the sand
Was heaving to engulf us,

The locusts raised a wind. Sunlight
   Scarcely filtered
Through, then, sudden decimator,

The car made paste-and-membrane
   Of their swarming,
Trophied where a hundred spanning

Wings and wrenched sky-hopping legs
      Had clung. We moved
Through famished miles, blind, remembered

Plagues as thick and foul about us.
      Reaching town, I
Hosed the car down for a day,

Then sold it. Today whenever
      I think of her,
Locusts, locusts, break around me.

Objet d'Art

The copper bowl I keep
      Tobacco
In is thick with nightingales

And roses, up to the
      Minaret
Its lid, incised so-so.

I no longer smoke in
      Company,
It seems indecent:

Reminded by those birds
      And flowers
Of a botched renown,

A Persian I once
      Had for tea
Turned from it and wept.

Snows

I

All night thick flakes have fallen,
The street below lies smothered
    With the past.
One remembers other snows
    (Images
In snapshots framed by the chill
Edge), ablaze before the thaw.

II

Disburdenment is what mind seeks
Above all other riches,
    Disburdenment
Of little griefs gathered like drifts
Into each corner. I think of
    This as, shovel
Arcing wide, breath peopling the air,
I hurl slosh like diamonds at
    A snout of sun.

Trees

I

For five years now
I've caught you
At your tricks,

Marveling as you've
Stirred after the brown
Death, the white.

Envious, I watch
You where the
Words don't come—

Remembering
A quick flame,
The settling of ash.

II

All day the powersaws whir,
Sick trees come down, festering
    The walk with limbs.

The old street stretches to cornfields
Like an amputee. Above the
    Rip-tooth clamor

Of a long-awaited spring,
Birds wheel like exiles in
    A time of war.

Image

The house
Huge ugly plant
Peeling rotting
Around us
Making dark dark
Draining
Cutting off
It will see
Our end
Its floorboards
Sinking
To our dead weight

Memo to the Builder

... and then
After the roof goes up
Remember to lay the eave trough
Wide and deep. A run
For squirrels and a river
For my birds. You know, I'd rather

You made the trough
So, than have the rooftop
Tarred and shingled. Keep
It in mind, the trough.
Also I'm not so sure of glass
In every window. But let that pass.

Still—and there are
Reasons enough, believe me—
It would please no end to be
In and out together.
And how it would thrill me should a bird,
Learning our secret, make a whir-

ring thoroughfare
Of a room or two.
Forget the weather. To
Have the wild, the rare
Not only happen, mind, but
Be the normal is exactly what

I'm after. Now
You know. Perhaps you
Think I've made your job too
Light? Good. Throw
Caution to the beams. Build me a home
The living day can enter, not a tomb.

Crow

He is made giddy by the sun,
And is stupid enough to race
Its rise and fall, so that at dawn

One spots him lumbering across the
Winter sky, then perched like a heart
Within the skeletal tree.

Wherever he goes he carries
His stomach like a weapon,
And the small bird hungering flies

In his wake, hoping for a crumb
As the foul beak chews and caws
Together and the black wings climb.

Devourer of acres, he drops
On the puny scarecrow and plants
Tomorrow's morsel between the flaps

Of its straw-stuck coat. Nothing
Frightens him, the hawk will whirl
From what he swoops for, this king

Of field and fat metropolis.
And already taken over
From the eagle, he must replace

That ancient master of the sky
On escutcheon and dollar.
In this usurpation he

Most resembles us: image of
Our gutty need and power, he
Merits all our rubbish and our love.

Cormorant

Men speak lightly of frustration,
As if they'd invented it.

As if like the cormorant
Of Gifu, thick leg roped, a ring

Cutting into the neck, they dived
All night to the fish-swelled water

And flapped up with the catch lodged
In the throat, only to have

The fisher yank it out and toss
It gasping on a breathless heap.

Then to dive again, hunger
Churning in the craw, air just

Slipping by the throat-ring
To spray against the lungs.

And once more to be jerked back in
And have the fisher grab the spoil.

Men speak lightly of frustration,
And dim in the lantern light

The cormorant makes out the flash
Of fins and, just beyond,

The streamered boats of tourists
Rocking under *saké* fumes.

Jackal

That he springs from a hole
And sniffs along the pit
For garbage delectable

Is no distinction: this any
Dog can do. And does. That
He flies at man-smell, canny

At hiding in places made
For roaches and the smallest
Mice, is not so very odd.

The sharp dividing line,
What makes us think of him
As neither out nor in,

Neither wild nor tractable
Is, first of all, his bark
Which is the laugh of a fool

Pulled out at midnight from
A reeking bed, and then
The outlaw look of him

As caught in the flashlight's shine,
Thin legs straddling something foul,
He yelps and bolts the town.

The Squirrel

Gray fur to brown earth,
   The grasses clinging,
Eyes still bright, piercing

Through those topmost boughs
   Where, choked with nuts,
It clambered to the sun.

The rat has come to gnaw,
   The dog to sniff,
And I to meet my death:

Gray flesh to brown earth,
   The grasses clinging,
Eyes still bright, piercing

Through those tangled roots
   Where, crazed with fear,
I leapt from shade to shade.

The Liberator

Approaching the laboratory gate
He heard familiar squeals and, again,
Myriad rat's feet along maze-planks,
Then crows, yelps, mews: he was
Climbing the gangway of the Ark,
The Deluge boiling round his knees.

Entering, he glanced back where
The smashed glass door reflected head
And wobbly shins: the rest of him he
Must have left out in the drunken
Dark. Plucked on by cries of those he'd
Come to save, he passed frothed rows

Of test tubes, pickled embryos.
A swipe of the arm, and down they crashed,
Slicking the concrete floor. Still
The living urged him on: Out! Out!
It was a cry he'd learned to
Understand. When he reached the

Guinea pigs, unsnapped the toolbox
Lid and sheared the cage-wire, they licked,
All gratitude, the palm that
Offered crumbs. The rats, when sprung,

Scurried dizzily across the
Table strewn with cheese he'd cached

For weeks. And now, no longer
Running wild, the cocks, mongrels, cats
Fed beak by jowl together.
High above them on a stool, he
Smiled the smile of God, first
Work done, betrayals yet to come.

The Final Slope

Climbing the final slope
He thought of them below
Ledged with the rancid goats.
　　Two hundred feet to go,
Their envy snapping on the rope,

He spat into the sun.
Then the mountain threw him:
Like a butcher's beast he hung,
　　Lashed to a crazy limb,
By pride and the wind undone.

By pride and the wind undone,
Legs swinging far beneath,
He felt the goats and their kids
　　Nibbling at his feet,
And the sun's beak in his bone.

Lifeguard

All day they crush around his pedestal,
　　Whiteness smoking on the bone,
　　　　Lotioned fat

Of sacrifice. The sandgirls ogling up
    Like carp would shimmer gladly
      In his net.

You who lounge about them in this sweat,
    Enjoy while there is time what
      Soon must leap

To snare and snaring stay, to whelp across
    His strand a siege of castle
      Captains. Act

Before those waves, tall henchmen of his eyes,
    Cut in and drag the darlings
      To his arms.

And They Call This Living!

The sea that morning was as unruffled
As a tub of dirty water,
But we couldn't find the plug.
All right, we said, let it sit,
Let the gull keep dropping to the scum.

Then our son came running running
With one hand held up high. All right,
We said, let him dream a stained eyetooth
Right out of the Leviathan's jaw.
He's glad, and what have we got to lose?

And all right, we said, let the sun
Burn down at will. We'll furl
The striped umbrella and let it do
Its worst. For once, we said, accept
The ruddy show just as it's always been:

The sea as so much liquid having
Nowhere else to go, an eyetooth
Some old peddler fished from a nosebag

As a relic to be bragged at school
And the sun the navel of us all.

Then just as sure as we were
Sprawling there, a wind sprang up
To knock the sea for loops
And spin the fishers in their smacks,
And the eyetooth started shrinking.

All right, we said, grabbing the kid
And unfurling the striped umbrella.
All right, all right as the sunburn started
Itching and we buried the eyetooth
In the sand—next time we'll know better.

Son

I no longer please him; he's found heroes
Whose exploits, of whatever style or magnitude,
Outstrip my own. Swinging a bat, running,
Shooting, you'd expect to be surpassed.

But it's also in the poems he reads,
Thoughts he cannot quite decipher.
Sometimes I hate what's dragged him
From my knees to lour before me,

Lofty with idols left and right,
Denying the castoff what shouldn't
Be denied a dog. Well, we grow, move off,
Despising all that's kept us from

Those misted vales and outlands
Roamed by dragons and redolent of maidens
Until, all heroes fallen,
We steal back home to clasp the only

Certain thing: which is no longer there.

I. M. Jean Cocteau

Who would bury
What did not
    Exist?

A puff of opium
Held over
    Seventy

Years between
The fat cheeks of
    Paris,

Your expiration
Dizzies and
    Bereaves.

Paris

With fifty thousand daubers
To paint your face, you will never
Grow old, they say, with as many lovelies
Legging up your squares, you will
Always gratify, they say, O with your river
    And your bridges and your quays,
    The mind need never wander to the north,
The east, the west, nor settle in the azured south,
    They say.

Yet ask any two Frenchmen
Spawned on the cobbles of whatever
Dreary *arrondissement*, ask them at the hour
    The terraces are emptied of their tables,
The chairs piled high, the sidewalks scoured,
    And looking to the north, the east,
    The west, finally to the brilliant
South, they'll say *Merde!* and *Merde!* again. That's what
    They say.

Ah, to one spawned on the asphalt
Of whatever American city, it is sweetest comfort
To know that, stripped of the décor, your gargoyles
          Pulled down (O hear the tourists sobbing in the choir!),
Bereft of the fifty thousand palettes and the
                    Innumerable brushes that hide your face,
          You are no more ugly than that garish
Daughter who, after plying fabulously the Champs Elysées,
          They say,

                    Ended up, five years later
          Under a gaslight in Les Halles. *Zut alors!*
I'd rather be a banker in Duluth, with a Swede
          Wife and two cars in the garage, than a
Boulevardier with ten *sous* in the pocket, a head gone
                    Soft with dreaming north, east, west and south,
          And a kept bitch that cheers the porter in a
Greasy bed. *Mon Dieu! c'est triste la vie, n'est-ce pas?*
          They say.

At Virgil's Tomb

The bus stops just outside the gate
          Where all day long
The kids retrieve their soccer ball.

I watch and wait (in Ravenna
          Your Florentine
Lay starred on every tourist's map,

And gendarmes' pikes, like gladioli,
          Blazed around him).
Now as the tour-bus honks below

I imagine another Beatrice
          Entreating you,
In glory's dream, to guide her lover

Through that flaming labyrinth.
          At last you speak:
"Tell him to live remembering you,

Say that long ago man's boot ground through
    Inferno's crust,
The world he made, and will not know."

Lines on an 18th C. Tapestry

It is a very pretty scene:
    As in a picture by Watteau,
The lovers seem about
    To strip themselves of all
Stiff finery and teach the faun

That stamps within the wood
    What violence a parcel
Of gallants bestirred, can wreak
    Upon a summer's greensward frail
With damsels of the blood.

On a damask stained with wine
    The ribboned marmosets devour
Such nibbled fruits and broken cakes
    That, envious in the wing-bright air,
The starlings cluster to complain.

His face uplifted to the sky,
    A lackey strums a mandolin,
But how should they attend harsh strings
    Who hear the song of flesh and bone
Stealing through their finery?

The Dream

He entered a zoo of reptiles
    Uncaged but chained,
Each with familiar face,
    Voice, claim on him.
The sunlight flashed off
    Scaly backs, earth
Clung to slimed jaws, the path wove
    Through and round them
From entrance to far wall—
    Dark, uneven.
But what most astonished as
    He passed the beasts
Was the cunning in the chains:
    Try as they might,
Muscles heaping, to claw beyond
    His shadow, which
Torn to strips of earth
    Was flung aside,
They could not. However single and
    Intense their claim,
However paws struck out, he passed
    Them unafraid:
Those chains rang solidly where they'd been
    Pegged in concrete.
His peace was like that of
    The tamer who,
After years of waltzing
    With the same cats,
Could lie for hours, head
    Between their fangs.
When he slipped the last of them,
    He came upon
A harem lined up in scale
    Of nakedness,
Faces like those one sees in
    Northern cities
Sharp at noon when shops and offices
    Debouch onto
The churning streets for sandwiches and
    Coffee. The first
Seemed very proper, and in one

Or another
He recognized a classmate
    For whom he'd itched,
Head in arms, eyes swung back
    And climbing thighs
And into panties like sacks
    Of tropic fruit.
Yet unlike the reptiles these made no
    Move toward him.
They tried to win him
    With demureness,
Never mind as he strode on the ripped
    Skirts, blouses slashed
To midriffs. He knew them all,
    just as they were,
With his lost fantastic eyes that were
    Always peering
Through and far beyond. And now it
    Was only fair
To pick one out and, he supposed,
    Save her from him
Whose chains would be the first to
    Give. Like a vain
Commander he went slowly by
    The lot, pinching
Here, patting there, then stood before
    The last of all,
Who posed, small hands raising
    Breasts, his mother's.
He rushed off, cheated, muttering,
    The smell so sharp
He must escape at once,
    And damn the lot.
At the wall the roaring
    Swelled where the beasts
Were strained and pawing at
    His back, the clang
Of chains like knells in
    A year of plague.
But the gate had disappeared.
    He groped along
The wall, which was horny to
    The touch and patched

With scales that formed
  Footholds, handgrips.
He leapt and slowly mounted,
  Fingers oozing,
Until at last he stared down at the
  Sea. The roaring
Ceased. He dived and woke to blackness.

Vogue

Your women are judged beautiful:
Their underarms are hairless, legs
  And netherzones.

Clamped to their breasts are tiny
Rubber shields and, circling low,
  Those sheering walls

No arrow yet has pierced, only
Gold pulls down. Your women
  Go unrivaled:

Impenetrable as fortresses
They line those cold medieval streets
  No charger dares.

How you must weep to see them giving
Suck, your daughters, to dolls
  Of flesh and blood.

Christ of Pershing Square

"I can prove it!" the madman cried
And clutched my wrist. "Feel where the nails
Went in! By God, I bear them still!"

Half amused, I shrugged and let him
Press the hand against his suture:
"All right," I said, "they cut you up."

Suddenly those fingers grasped
A hammer, it was I had hoisted
The cross his flung arms formed there.

"Yet," I whispered, "there remains
The final proof—forgiveness."
He spat into my face and fled.

This happened in Los Angeles
Six months ago. I see him still,
White blood streaming, risen from

Cancerous sheets to walk a Kingdom.

Lament for Weldon Kees

Could we have known that torrid night
A book of yours would sell
For eighteen dollars, we might

Have gotten a little drunker.
Weldon, where the blazes are you?
I can't help thinking of your

Wife, the lovely way she
Had of listening, holding her
Pride in you like a virginity.

We talked of poems, your "Robinson,"
And then you shuffled back
To slap some more paint down,

The canvas flat upon the table,
Under a light so fierce I thought
The paint would run. You didn't call

It that, but painting was your hackwork,
And surely the hope of poet's ease
Held you there from dark to dark,

The gin beside you on a stool.
I was green as grass, and you
My first live poet. What a bloody fool

You must have thought me! But it
Wasn't your praise I wanted then,
And thank Christ you knew that.

Just to be with you, and talk,
And drink your gin was what I'd
Come for. I left your room to walk

The city ragged, knowing at last
That poets were quite human.
Later, when I heard that you were lost,

Your car found parked too near the bridge,
I wondered which of us had left it there.
By then I too was hanging from the edge.

The Cannery

In summer this town is full of rebels
Come up from Tennessee to shell the peas.

And wetbacks roam the supermarts, making
A Tijuana of the drab main street.

The Swedes and Poles who work at Wurlitzer,
And can't stand music, are all dug in:

Doors are bolted, their pretty children warned,
Where they wait for the autumnal peace.

At night the cannery's like a train,
A runaway, cans flung up like clinkers.

Sometimes on an evening hot as Southland
When even fear won't keep the windows down,

One hears the drawl of Tennessee, the quick
Laugh of Mexico in the empty streets.

To an Astronaut

Drink up! The night's a cave
Whose mouth, the moon,
Wastes to a hair's-breadth
Then is lost in clouds.

And who are you to climb
Such steeps of sky, where
Huge on hills of frozen
Light, the gods are ravening

And jealous angels, wakened
By your knocking, gather
Hailstones and the chunkiest
Pips of heaven to pelt

You as you rise? Already
Certain saints pray for you
In futurity, confused
By an image pierced

With the silver metals
Of its fall to martyrdom.

And those departed ones
Who shaped you lovingly

For this one terrible role
(And thereby entered Paradise)
Kneel in readiness
With wreaths and mute hosannas

At the icy tombstone
Each has wept for you.
Drink up! I say.
The gods roar, ravening.

Speech to the Shapers

They are wrong who think the end will be
Violent, rank alarmists who have
Visions of bombs bursting east and west
Together, leaving their hillocks of

Dead. Or who sniff already in the
Wind the poisons that will circle and
Devour. They have not lived enough who
See great armies joined along a strand

By nothing more than the bayonets
They'd stabbed into each other's innards,
With, to complete the savage picture,
Vultures and, moored with flesh, the buzzards.

And what must one really think of those
Who leap from Bibles reciting Doom,
When not only every Doom so far
Recited has failed, like rain, to come

But even the callowest Sunday
Schooler grins? The end will steal upon
Us as an average day, sometime between
Breakfast and lunch, while Father is down

At the office, Junior playing ball
And Mother is choosing lambchops at
The butcher's. Unannounced, it will drop
From a cloudless sky, or like a cut

In the power take us by surprise,
With all the lights snuffed out together.
But far more than the lights will go out,
And whatever's wrong will not appear

To be wrong, and it will have begun not
The day before, or now, or even
A thousand years ago. There's the rub.
We'll never know what hit us where, or when.

Steve Crawley

Why whenever they mention Hawaii
Do I think of you, and not the hula
Girls or orchids shrill against the blue?
Why when they send postcards of tourists tense
Around a burning pig, leis like collars
On a brace of hounds, do I see you flung
Across the earthfloor of that tent again,
Brains like macaroni puddled at the ear?

Steve Crawley, we found her letter crushed
Between the oilcan and the rosary
On your cot, and thought we understood,
But what puzzles still is this: what were you
Doing in that cathouse line, all brass
And itch, the night before the letter came?

The Pit

Twenty years. I still remember
The sun-blown stench, and the pit
At least two hundred yards from
The cove we'd anchored guns in.
They were blasting at the mountains,
The beach was nearly ours.

The smell kept leaking back.
I thought of garbage cans
Behind chopsuey restaurants
Of home, strangely appealing on
A summer's night, meaning another
Kind of life. Which made the difference.

When the three of us, youngest in
The crew, were handed poles and told
To get the deadmen underground
Or join them, we saw it a sullen
Sort of lark. And lashed to trees,
The snipers had us dancing.

Ducks for those vultures in the boughs,
Poles poking through the powder-
Bitten grass, we zigzagged
Toward the pit as into
The arse of death, the wittiest
Of us said but did not laugh.

At last we reached it, half full
Of sand and crawling. We clamped
Nose, mouth, wrenched netted helmets
To the chin, yet poles probed forward
Surgically, touching for spots
The maggots had not jelled.

Somehow we got the deadmen under,
Along with empty lobster tins,
Bottles, gear and ammo. Somehow
We plugged the pit and slipped back
To the guns. Then for days
We had to helmet bathe downwind.

I stuck my pole, clean end high,
Behind the foxhole, a kind of
Towelpeg and a something more.
I'd stare it out through jungle haze,
And wonder. Ask anyone who
Saw it: nobody won that war.

From *Afterimages: Zen Poems
of Shinkichi Takahashi* (1970)

A Wood in Sound

The pinetree sways in the smoke,
Which streams up and up.
There's a wood in sound.

My legs lose themselves
Where the river mirrors daffodils
Like faces in a dream.

A cold wind and the white memory
Of a sasanqua.
Warm rain comes and goes.

I'll wait calmly on the bank
Till the water clears
And willows start to bud.

Time is singed on the debris
Of air raids.
Somehow, here and now, I am another.

Aching of Life

There must be something better,
But I'm satisfied just as I am.

Monkeys sport deep in the forest,
Fish shoot up the mountain stream.

If there's change, there's also repose—
Which soon must suffer change.

Along the solar orbit of the night,
I feel life's constant aching:

Smack in the middle of the day,
I found moonlight between a woman's legs.

Snow Wind

There's nothing more to see:
Snow in the nandin's leaves
And, under it, the red-eyed
Rabbit lies frozen.

I'll place everything on
Your eyeballs, the universe.
There's nothing more to see:
Nandin berries are red, snow white.

The rabbit hopped twice in the cool
Breeze and everyone disappeared,
Leaving the barest scent.
The horizon curves endlessly

And now there's no more light
Around the rabbit's body.
Suddenly your face
Is large as the universe.

Canna

A red canna blooms,
While between us flickers
A death's head, dancing there
Like a pigmy or tiny ball.

We try to catch it—
Now it brushes my hands,
Now dallies with her feet.

She often talks of suicide.
Scared, I avoid her cold face.

Again today she spoke
Of certain premonitions.
How can I possibly
Save this woman's life?

Living as if dead, I shall
Give up my own. She must live.

Time

Time like a lake breeze
Touched his face,
All thought left his mind.

One morning the sun, menacing,
Rose from behind a mountain,
Singeing—like hope—the trees.

Fully awakened, he lit his pipe
And assumed the sun-inhaling pose:
Time poured down—like rain, like fruit.

He glanced back and saw a ship
Moving towards the past. In one hand
He gripped the sail of eternity,

And stuffed the universe into his eyes.

The Pink Sun

White petals on the black earth,
Their scent filling her nostrils.

Breathe out and all things swell—
Breathe in, they shrink.

Let's suppose she suddenly has four legs—
That's far from fantastic.

I'll weld ox hoofs onto her feet—
Sparks of the camellia's sharp red.

Wagging her pretty little tail,
She's absorbed in kitchenwork.

Look, she who just last night
Was a crone is girl again,

An alpine rose blooming on her arm.
High on a Himalayan ridge

The great King of Bhutan
Snores in the pinkest sun.

Thistles

Thistles bloomed in the vast moonlit
Cup of the Mexican sands.

Thistles bloomed on the round hillock
Of a woman's heart.

The stained sea was choked with thistles,
Sky stowed away in thistle stalks.

Thistles, resembling a male corpse, bloomed
Like murex from a woman's side.

At the thorny root of a yellow cactus plant
A plucked pigeon crouched,

And off in the distance a dog whimpered,
As if swallowing hot air.

Rat on Mount Ishizuchi

Snow glitters on the divine rocks
At the foot of Mount Ishizuchi.
Casting its shadow on the mountain top,
A rat flies off.

At the back of the sun,
Where rats pound rice into cakes,
There's a cavity like a mortar pit.

A flyer faster than an airplane,
That's the sparrow.
Mount Ishizuchi, too, flies at a devilish speed,
Ten billion miles a second,
From everlasting to everlasting.

Yet, because there's no time,
And always the same dusk,
It doesn't fly at all:
The peak of Mount Ishizuchi
Has straightened the spine
Of the Island of Futana.

Because there's no space
The airplane doesn't move an inch:
The sun, the plane boarded by the rat,
Are afloat in the sparrow's dream.

Burning Oneself to Death

That was the best moment of the monk's life.
Firm on a pile of firewood
With nothing more to say, hear, see,
Smoke wrapped him, his folded hands blazed.

There was nothing more to do, the end
Of everything. He remembered, as a cool breeze

Streamed through him, that one is always
In the same place, and that there is no time.

Suddenly a whirling mushroom cloud rose
Before his singed eyes, and he was a mass
Of flame. Globes, one after another, rolled out,
The delighted sparrows flew round like fire balls.

Back Yard

The sky clears after rain,
Yellow roses glistening in the light.
Crossing two thresholds, the cat moves off.

Your back is overgrown with nandin leaves.
How awkward your gait!
Like a chicken on damp leaves.
Your necktie, made from skin
Of a tropical fighting fish,
Is hardly subdued. Your yolk-colored
Coat will soon be dyed
With blood again, like a cock's crest.

Let your glances pierce
Like a hedgehog's spines,
I reject them. I can't imagine
What would happen if our glances met.

One day I'll pulverize you.
Now you're scratching
In the bamboo roots, famished.
Watch it—I'll toss you down a hole.

With your cockspurs you kick off
Mars, earth, mankind,
All manner of things, then
Pick over them with your teeth.

Atomic horses bulge through
The pores of a peach-like girl.
The persimmon's leaves are gone again.

The Pipe

While I slept it was all over,
Everything. My eyes, squashed white,
Flowed off toward dawn.

There was a noise,
Which, like all else, spread and disappeared:
There's nothing worth seeing, listening for.

When I woke, everything seemed cut off.
I was a pipe, still smoking,
Which daylight would knock empty once again.

Crow

The crow, spreading wide wings,
Flapped lazily off.
Soon her young will be doing the same,
Firm wings rustling.

It's hard to tell the male
Crow from the female,
But their love, their mating
Must be fresh as their flight.

Asleep in a night train,
I felt my hat fly off.
The crow was lost in mist,
The engine ploughed into the sea.

White Flower

One flower, my family and I,
And I but a petal.
I grasp a hoe in one hand,
Wife and child by the other.

It wasn't I who drove that stake
Into the earth, then pulled it out.
I'm innocent—rather we are,
Like that white cloud above.

I stretch out my right hand: nothing.
I raise my left: nobody.
A white flower opens,
And now I stand apart

While, above, a bomber soars.
My family and I are buried alive.
I'm a handful of earth.
Untraceable.

Mummy

Resuscitated
By the kiss of a bat
On its papyrus mouth
And the Nile's spring thrust,
The mummy arose amidst
The jolting pillars
And strode from the cave,
Followed by a throng of bats.

Tripping on a pyramid step,
The mummy was landed upon
By a bat, a sarcophagus lid,
Who, by patting its head with her wing,
Unwound the mummy's cloth,
Dipped it in the Nile,

Then wrapped it round herself
From claw-tips to shoulders.
She lay down—a mummy.

Tail up, the sphinx came
To sniff her all over,
But the bat was fast asleep.
How many centuries have slipped by?
The dam's dried up,
This once submerged temple
Stands again,
Its stone birds
Have once more taken flight.

Red Waves

A cat, a black-white tabby out of nowhere,
Licks its back at the water's edge:
Perhaps—with that bit of metal dangling
From her middle—a space cat,
Readying to fly off again.

But how to ask her? I opened my hand, wide,
just in front of her face, at which
She flipped over, legs up and pointing
Toward the sea in the pose of a "beckoning cat."

The sea obliged: she was carried off
Bobbing on the waves. Was she drowned?
I asked myself over and over,
Alone for hours on the moonlit beach.

Suddenly a red parasol came rolling
Toward me—the cat's? It danced along
The windless shore, with me chasing full tilt.
I didn't have a chance. Come daybreak
I spotted the parasol rising above a rock:
The sun, blinding! Red waves reached my ankles.

Destruction

The universe is forever falling apart—
No need to push the button,
It collapses at a finger's touch:
Why, it barely hangs on the tail of a sparrow's eye.

The universe is so much eye secretion,
Hordes leap from the tips
Of your nostril hairs. Lift your right hand:
It's in your palm. There's room enough
On the sparrow's eyelash for the whole.

A paltry thing, the universe:
Here is all strength, here the greatest strength.
You and the sparrow are one
And, should he wish, he can crush you.
The universe trembles before him.

Disclosure

The sparrow sleeps, thinking of nothing.
Meanwhile the universe has shrunk to half.
He's attached by a navel string, swimming
In a sea of fluid, amniotic, slightly bitter.

The center is "severance"—no sound at all—
Until the navel string is snapped. All of which
Was told by her as she sat astride Pegasus,
The poet on a circuit of the universe.

The sparrow came at her, bill like a sword,
And suddenly from her buttocks—the sun!
The sparrow carried the stained sheets
To the moon. On drawing the clouds apart,

He discovered the cold corpse of Mars.
Not once had he disclosed the secrets of his life.

What Is Moving

When I turned to look back
Over the waters
The sky was birdless.

Men *were, are* born.
Do I still live? I ask myself,
Munching a sweet potato.

Don't smell of death,
Don't cast its shadow.
Any woman when I glance her way,
Looks down,
Unable to stand it.
Men, as if dead,
Turn up the whites of their eyes.

Get rid of those trashy ideas—
The same thing
Runs through both of us.
My thought moves the world:
I move, it moves.
I crook my arm, the world's crooked.

The Peach

A little girl under a peach tree,
Whose blossoms fall into the entrails
Of the earth.

There you stand, but a mountain may be there
Instead; it is not unlikely that the earth
May be yourself.

You step against a plate of iron and half
Your face is turned to iron. I will smash
Flesh and bone

And suck the cracked peach. She went up the mountain
To hide her breasts in the snowy ravine.
Women's legs

Are more or less alike. The leaves of the peach tree
Stretch across the sea to the end of
The continent.

The sea was at the little girl's beck and call.
I will cross the sea like a hairy
Caterpillar

And catch the odor of your body.

Quails

It is the grass that moves, not the quails.
Weary of embraces, she thought of
Committing her body to the flame.

When I shut my eyes, I hear far and wide
The air of the Ice Age stirring.
When I open them, a rocket passes over a meteor.

A quail's egg is complete in itself,
leaving not room enough for a dagger's point.
All the phenomena in the universe: myself.

Quails are supported by the universe
(I wonder if that means subsisting by God).
A quail has seized God by the neck

With its black bill, because there is no
God greater than a quail.
(Peter, Christ, Judas: a quail.)

A quail's egg: idle philosophy in solution.
(There is no wife better than a quail.)
I dropped a quail's egg into a cup for buckwheat noodles,

And made havoc of the Democratic Constitution.
Split chopsticks stuck in the back, a quail husband
Will deliver dishes on a bicycle, anywhere.

The light yellow legs go up the hill of Golgotha.
Those quails who stood on the rock, became the rock!
The nightfall is quiet, but inside the congealed exuviae

Numberless insects zigzag, on parade.

Horse

Young girls bloom like flowers.
Unharnessed, a horse trots
Round its driver who
Grasps it by a rope.

Far off a horse is going round and round
In a square plot.

Not miserable, not cheerful either,
The bay horse is prancing,
Shaking its head, throwing up its legs
By turn: it is not running.

But there are no spectators
In what looks like an amphitheater.

White cherry petals fall like snowflakes
In the wind. All at once,
Houses, people vanish, into silence.
Nothing moves. Streetcars, buses, are held back
Silently. Quiet, everything.
All visible things become this nothingness.

The horse's bones—beautiful in their gray sheen.
A horse is going round and round,
Dancing now, with *joie de vivre*,
Under the cliff of death.

Collapse

Time oozed from my pores,
Drinking tea
I tasted the seven seas.

I saw in the mist formed
Around me
The fatal chrysanthemum, myself.

Its scent choked, and as I
Rose, squaring
My shoulders, the earth collapsed.

Sun

Stretched in the genial sun
The mountain snake
Tickled its length along the rock.

The wind rustled the sunshine,
But the snake,
Fully uncoiled, was calm.

Fifty thousand years ago!
Later the same sun
Blazed across the pyramids,

Now it warms my chest.
But below, through
Shattered rock, the snake

Thrusts up its snout, fangs
Flicking at my thoughts
Strewn about the rocks like violets.

It's you, faces cut like triangles,
Have kept the snake alive!
The pavement's greened with leaves.

Words

I don't take your words
Merely as words.
Far from it.

I listen
To what makes you talk—
Whatever that is—
And me listen.

Rain

The rain keeps falling,
Even in dreams.
The skull leaks badly.

There's a constant dripping
Down the back.
The rain, which no one

Remembers starting,
Keeps falling,
Even on the finest days.

Bream

What's land? What's water?
In the window of the florist
Swims the big-eyed bream,
Between dahlias, chrysanthemums.

So you're alone? Well, forget
Others, keep talking to yourself.
Past the hydrangea leaves
Sways the scaly bream-mass.

History? Look between
The dry leaves of the sardine
Paper. Oops! the anemone's
Finally snagged a scale,

And flowering on a tulip stem,
The bream's tail and fin!
Why fear? What do you know
Of what happens after death?

Just remember to pierce
The cactus through your Christmas hat.
Brushed by trumpet lilies, roses,
The bream opens/shuts his mouth.

The Position of the Sparrow

The sparrow has cut the day in half:
Afternoons—yesterday's, the day after tomorrow's—
Layer the white wall.
Those of last year, and next year's too,
Are dyed into the wall—see them?—
And should the wall come down,
Why, those afternoons will remain,
Glimmering, just as they are, through time.
(That was a colorless realm where,
Nevertheless, most any color could well up.)

Just as the swan becomes a crow,
So everything improves—everything:
No evil *can* persist, and as to things,
Why, nothing is unchangeable.
The squirrel, for instance, is on the tray,
Buffalos lumber through African brush,
The snail wends along the wall,
Leaving a silver trail.
The sparrow's bill grips a pomegranate seed:
Just anything can resemble a lens, or a squirrel.

Because the whole is part, there's not a whole,
Anywhere, that is not part.
And all those happenings a billion years ago,
Are happening now, all around us: time.
Indeed this morning the sparrow hopped about
In that nebulous whirlpool
A million light years hence.
And since the morning is void,
Anything can be. Since mornings
A billion years from now are nothingness,
We can behold them.
The sparrow stirs,
The universe moves slightly.

Deck

If time is but a stream flowing from past to future,
Why, it's nothing more than sardine guts!
If all is carried away by it,
Then everything is seaweed along a desolate strand!
Has this stream no end at all?
Then there ought to be an unmapped sea around it.

The tide moves at its own sweet will,
Yet whether it moves or not—who cares?
Still, an absolutely immobile ship is by the quay:
Should its anchor drop to the depths of time,
We'll have had it, the harbor will dry up.

A sailor goes ashore, walking along
With existence in the palm of his hand.
With nothing under him,
His tapering toes extend,
Then—like a meteor—disappear.

The sailor is free to go anywhere,
No deck is bigger than his hand.

Mascot

Somebody is breathing inside me—
Birds, the very earth.

The ocean's in my chest. Walking,
I always throw myself down.

Newssheets, a puppy were dancing in the wind—
Trucks rushed by,

Empty trucks stout enough to carry the earth
On their puncture-proof tires.

The instant I raised my hand to wave,
I was nowhere.

The puppy was sprawled out on its belly,
Run over—again, again.

You're a badger, I'll bet, posing as a mascot
With that moonlit tie

And, sticking from your pocket, night's flower.

Stitches

My wife is always knitting, knitting:
Not that I watch her,
Not that I know what she thinks.

(Awake till dawn
I drowned in your eyes—
I must be dead:
Perhaps it's the mind that stirs.)

With that bamboo needle
She knits all space, piece by piece,
Hastily hauling time in.

Brass-cold, exhausted,
She drops into bed and,
Breathing calmly, falls asleep.

Her dream must be deepening,
Her knitting coming loose.

Snail

The snail crawls over blackness.

Just now, in the garden,
A solid lump of snow
Slipped from the zinc roof
To behead the nandin.

Make it snappy!

In full view a stalk has been
Torn off:
Let the wind rage over the earth,
He is unaware.

His head flies to the end
Of the world,
His body is tossed
Into the ash can.

Could it be that he's the falling snow?

Fish

I hold a newspaper, reading.
Suddenly my hands become cow ears,
Then turn into Pusan, the South Korean port.

Lying on a mat
Spread on the bankside stones,
I fell asleep.
But a willow leaf, breeze-stirred,
Brushed my ear.
I remained just as I was,
Near the murmurous water.

When young there was a girl
Who became a fish for me.
Whenever I wanted fish
Broiled in salt, I'd summon her.
She'd get down on her stomach
To be sun-cooked on the stones.
And she was always ready!

Alas, she no longer comes to me.
An old benighted drake,
I hobble homeward.
But look, my drake feet become horse hoofs!
Now they drop off
And, stretching marvelously,
Become the tracks of the Tokaido Railway Line.

Body

My body's been torn to pieces,
Limbs sway in the wind
Like those of the persimmon,
Thick with blue leaves.

Suddenly a butterfly,
My eyeballs spots

On its wings,
Takes off, brilliant.

Future's circled by a crumbling
Earthen wall, and the dog's
Pregnant with earth,
Nipples of its swollen teats

Sharp as lead in a red pencil.
As I rushed through flame
An airplane passed between
My legs. Sky's my body.

Afterimages

The volcanic smoke of Mount Aso
Drifted across the sea, white ash
Clinging to mulberry leaves
And crowning the heads of sparrows.

An open-mouthed lava crocodile;
A sparrow like a fossil sprig,
The moon filling its eyes;
A colossal water lizard stuck to a dead tree,
Its headland tail quaking.

A cloud floats in my head—beautiful!
When the sparrow opens its eyes,
Nothing but rosy space. All else gone.

Don't tell me that tree was red—
The only thing that moved, ever closer,
Was a girl's nose. All mere afterimages.

Water, coldness itself, flows underfoot.

The sparrow, eyes half closed, lay in an urn
In the pit. Now it fans up. The earth's
Fiery column is nearly extinguished.

Awakening (1973)

Awakening

Homage To Hakuin, Zen Master, 1685-1768

I

Shoichi brushed the black
on thick.
His circle held a poem
like buds
above a flowering bowl.

Since the moment of my
pointing,
this bowl, an "earth device,"
holds
nothing but the dawn.

II

A freeze last night, the window's
laced ice flowers, a meadow drifting
from the glacier's side. I think of Hakuin:

"Freezing in an icefield, stretched
thousands of miles in all directions,
I was alone, transparent, and could not move."

Legs cramped, mind pointing
like a torch, I cannot see beyond
the frost, out nor in. And do not move.

III

I balance the round stone
     in my palm,
turn it full circle,

slowly, in the late sun,
     spring to now.
Severe compression,

like a troubled head,
        stings my hand.
It falls. A small dust rises.

IV

Beyond the sycamore
dark air moves
westward—

smoke, cloud, something
wanting a name.
Across the window,

my gathered breath,
I trace
a simple word.

V

My daughter gathers shells
where thirty years before
I'd turned them over, marveling.

I take them from her,
make, at her command,
the universe. Hands clasped,

marking the limits of
a world, we watch till sundown
planets whirling in the sand.

VI

Softness everywhere,
snow a smear,
air a gray sack.

Time. Place. Thing.
Felt between
skin and bone, flesh.

VII

I write in the dark again,
rather by dusk-light,
and what I love about

this hour is the way the trees
are taken, one by one,
into the great wash of darkness.

At this hour I am always happy,
ready to be taken myself,
fully aware.

Away

Here I go again,
want to be somewhere else—
feet tramping under the desk,

I study travel brochures,
imagine monastic Hiltons,
the caravansary of my past.

Apples, cheese, a hunk of bread,
the road: what'll it be today?
I ask myself: the Seine,

Isfahan bazaar, three claps
of the hand, and Yamaguchi,
Takayama-roshi shouting—

Down, down, and breathe!
My feet go faster faster,
suddenly fly off.

Calm, breathing slowly,
I bow to Master Takayama
who smiles all the way from Japan.

Museum Guards (London)

I

He smokes against the wall
blowing rings where Moore's giants
escape through the holes

in themselves. He is small among
them, and his cigarette, the one
live thing, fizzles in the rain.

II

You would have understood what made
the guard leap from his chair
and, pointing at your saints,

cry out in Italian—
"What am I doing here?" Carlo Crivelli,
what is wrong with this world?

III

He watches us watching, weary,
cough straightening his slouch.
Seven years facing the Watteaus.

Life's no picnic. Ask him, the crippled
one who used to whisper shyly
that he was an artist, waiting for the break.

Hyde Park Sunday

Suddenly the bronzed Spaniard,
yellow bandanna on his forehead,
left his companions with a leap—
perfect somersault—then cartwheeled
past the lovers on the grass.

The sprawlers gaped, on Speakers' Corner
there was silence, those angry men
turned blessed, forgiving—
so much pure energy expended for nothing,
for absolutely nothing.

Elegy for a Long-Haired Student

He called at four a.m.: about to fly
to Mao, he had to know the Chinese word
for peace. Next day he was dead.

"Such dreams were bound for madness,"
I told his mourners. "He was too good
for this world." "He would have wanted you,"

they said. "*You* understood." Bearing
his body to the grave, I saw the long red hair
he could not stop from coiling round

their throats: Elks, Legionnaires.
Unmocked now, it would grow. As we lay
him down, I spoke that word for peace.

South

Walking at night, I always return to
    the spot beyond
the cannery and cornfields where

a farmhouse faces south among tall trees.
    I dream a life
there for myself, everything happening

in an upper room: reading in sunlight,
    talk, over wine,
with a friend, long midnight poems swept

with stars and a moon. And nothing
    being savaged,
anywhere. Having my fill of that life,

I imagine a path leading south
    through corn and wheat,
to the Gulf of Mexico! I walk

each night in practice for that walk.

Noon Report

Though yesterday, as forecast,
shot by on a wind
from the northwest,
promising nothing much,

this afternoon the blue
limbs of the sky
hang still. Up there,
as usual, something's

concocting tomorrow
which, despite the mess
we're bound to make of it,
should arrive on time.

Confession

When with my stuffed beginner's hook
    lodged in his lip
the small-mouth bass shot up
and almost ditched the rowboat, I jerked
    the flyrod high.

Caught there, eye to eye, we flashed
    together in
the sun, flyrod ablaze
between us—midspace, midlife—
    then the plunging.

I dream him down there still,
    crawdad sucked to
bone, flyrod clicking on the lakebed
where, shrunk from the anchored hulls,
    he slowly spins.

Fishing with My Daughter in Miller's Meadow

You follow, dress held high above
    the fresh manure,
missing your doll, scolding Miller's horses

for being no gentlemen where they graze
    in morning sun.
You want the river, quick, I promised you back there,

and all those fish. I point to trees where
    water rides low
banks, slopping over in the spring,

and pull you from barbed wire protecting corn
    the size of you
and gaining fast on me. To get you in the meadow

I hold the wire high, spanning a hand across
     your freckled back.
At last we make the river, skimmed with flies,

you help me scoop for bait. I give you time
     to run away,
then drop the hook. It's fish I think

I'm after, you I almost catch, in up to knees,
     sipping minnowy
water. Well, I hadn't hoped for more.

Going back, you heap the creel with phlox and marigolds.

Storm

The green horse of the tree
bucks in the wind
as lightning hits beyond.
We will ride it out together,
or together fall.

After the Storm

Slick of water on
the picnic table,
beaded lawnchairs,

street steaming in
the early heat.
Thrumming underground,

dead grass will spring
again. Half way up
the maple's trunk

the first-born squirrel's
nose. The bluejay,
like a startled eye,

darts from branch to branch.

Twister

Waiting the twister which touched down
a county north, leveled a swath
of homes, taking twenty lives,

we sit in battered chairs, southwest
corner of the basement, listen
to the radio warnings through

linoleum and creaky floorboards
of the kitchen overhead. We are
like children in a spooky film,

ghosts about to enter at the door.
I try to comfort them, though
most afraid, *Survival Handbook*

open on my lap. Around our
piled up junk cobwebs sagged with flies,
though early spring. A trunk with French Line

stickers, paint flaked in our defective
furnace heat, a stack of dishes
judged too vulgar for our guests,

sled with rusted runners, cockeyed pram
and broken dolls, Christmas trinkets
we may use again, some boards kept

mainly for the nails. I watch my wife,
son, daughter, wondering what we're up to,
what's ahead. We listen, ever

silent, for the roar out of the west,
whatever's zeroing in with terror
in its wake. The all-clear sounds,

a pop song hits above. Made it
once again. We shove the chairs
against the wall, climb into the light.

The Cherry

February: the season grips—
    heavy—the chomped
stalks in Miller's field
    across the way.

Wind comes level, spurred by
    western counties,
and horses our daughter watched
    all summer long

shiver in woodland now. Below,
    piled branches
downed by the storm of mid-December
    shift in the gusts.

We have waited a month for the city
    to cart them off—
it's been so cold the ice that
    let the storm strip

clean, has scarcely thawed. The day
    those branches split
I had to axe the cherry to its roots.
    Our girl, sulking

out of range, held tight to twigs.

Here and Now

Sunglasses upturned
on the picnic table,
where I try to write,

catch my reflection
square—sweaty, vain.
What's the use?

Hear a knocking
at the front. No muse,
a salesman

from the Alcoa
Aluminum Company
inspired by the siding

of our rented house.

Morning

I lie late where
sunlight floods the curtain,
tracing dust lines here and there.

I want to remain
floating on the sheet,
a whitecap bearing me to shores I need,

a chosen world
where no one waits
and nothing cares. Soon I shall draw

the curtain
on the window tree,
quick birds among the leaf-trace.

They build around
me, everything waits
to happen. The paper on the desk

is like a distant
sunlit pool, my pen
an indolent bather, weary of all.

Black Partridge Woods, before a Reading

Soon words, words, words, now silence
        in the woods
of this blue-collar town.

Noon. A freight rocks rails
        lumbering
toward Chicago. Factory whistles,

everywhere, at once. Where is
        the poet
who named these woods? Mud on my shoes,

lost for an hour with the children
        of Lemont,
Illinois, I talk of partridges and poems.

Heat

Hundred degrees.
After four days
we are the sprawling
dead. The fingers

of the fan can't
claw through heat
piled up like earth.
Garbage steams

and buzzes—a page
from Dante's Hell.
Air burns the tips
of maple leaves.

Where's the rainmaker?
Somewhere black
clouds must form—
then why not here?

Summer

My neighbor frets about his lawn,
and he has reasons—
dandelions, crabgrass, a passing dog.

He scowls up at my maple, rake
clogged and trembling,
as its seeds spin down—

not angels, moths, but paratroopers
carried by the wind,
planting barricades along his eaves.

He's on the ladder now, scaring
the nibbling squirrels,
scattering starlings with his water hose.

Thank God his aim is bad
or he'd have drowned
or B-B gunned the lot. Now he

shakes a fist of seeds at me
where I sit poeming
my dandelions, crabgrass and a passing dog.

I like my neighbor, in his way
he cares for me. Look what
I've given him—something to feel superior to.

No Hitter

By the seventh it was more than a ballgame,
I crushed the rosin-bag before each pitch.

Something said: this is it, either you make
it or you don't, all life long. Either they

hit you, or you get it by them, clean.
But they were there to do the same: either they

hit me or they don't. And it would last forever.
Balanced till the bottom of the ninth, we

grimly learned the score. Whoever pitied whom,
they hit me—my no-hitter was a rout.

It was relief I felt (and got)—that power
would have scared, or so I told myself.

White City

High on abandoned
rollercoaster tracks,
over Chicago,
a kite-tail in the wind,
we inched along the rotted
slats, proving ourselves
against the tug of earth.

Rivals' stones whizzing
by our ears, this was no
King-of-the-Mountain game,
we knew, as later on our knees
we worked our way below
with nothing in our hands,
not even stones.

My Daughter's Aquarium

You ask another question,
to be put off again, then
  walk away

so sad, I call you back.
It started out with birth—
  why? how? when?

From there, promised you
would hardly burst when
  that time came,

you moved on to greater perils—
beauty vanished, friends who
  always hurt.

All, things answerable, things
assurance turned to good. And
  now you're off

again, quickly from tank
to tank, passing the porpoise
  suspended

like a plastic Disney toy,
on the edge of tears,
  hating my

half answers to your questions,
blaming me as fish dart
  from your grasp.

I follow, then pull you out
into the autumn day when
  suddenly

you want to be in water,
threaten, above sobs, to
  swim away.

The Unknown Neighbor

The road you took to death
I traveled on, three hours before,
and made it safely home.

I hadn't met you, being me,
but often saw you home
from work, circled by kids

shrieking as you tossed
them up, again, again,
your wife tall in the doorway,

almost too tired to smile.
You were the perfect neighbor—
lawn mowing, leaf raking,

unborrowing—just so for
our town. And now your door
is shut, your family gone

five months since your death
to another husband, father.
Leaves pile high on lawn

and sidewalk, still throughout
the neighborhood fly rumors
of a widow's nights.

The Duckpond

I

Crocus, daffodil:
　　already the pond's
　　　　clear of ice

where, winter long,
    ducks and gulls
        slid for crusts.

People circle—
    pale, bronchitic,
        jostling behind dogs,

grope toward lawnchairs
    spread like islands
        on the grass.

Sunk there, they lift faces to the sun.

II

Good Friday.
    Ducks carry on,
        a day like any other.

Same old story:
    no one seems to care.
        A loudmouth

leader of a mangy host
    spiked to a cross,
        as blackbirds in certain

lands neighboring on
    that history are splayed
        on fences, warning

to their kind. A duck soars from the reeds.

III

Man and woman
    argue past the duckpond,
        his arms flailing,

she, head down—even
    by the fully budded
        cherry, clustered

lilac boughs. Not once
   do they forget
      their bitterness,

face the gift of morning
   ducks wake to
      in the reeds.

They have things to settle, and they will.

IV

On my favorite
   bench beside the roses
      I watch ducks

smoothing feathers,
   breathing it all in.
      Catching the headline

where the bird flits
   I'm reminded
      three men were shot up

at the moon. I turn
   back to the roses:
      what

if they don't make it? If they do?

V

Lying near the pond
   in fear of the stray
      dog that daily

roams the park,
   ducks know
      their limitations,

and the world's—
>how long it takes,
>>precisely,

to escape the paw thrusts
>of the dog,
>>who once again

swings round to chase his tail.

VI

Radio tower
>beyond the blossoms,
>>ducks

here in the pond,
>a connection
>>between them—

how did I discover
>this, and why?
>>Was it

the blue air? The bench
>moves beneath
>>us like a seesaw,

the pond sends news of the world.

VII

What becomes of things
>we make or do?
>>The Japanese lantern

or from across the pond
>beneath the trees
>>a drift

of voices cultured
    and remote: water
        will carry anything

that floats. The lantern
    maker, the couple
        chatting there

would be amazed to find themselves a poem.

VIII

When tail wagging
    in the breeze
        the duck pokes

bill into the pondbed,
    keeps it there,
        my daughter thinks

him fun—he is, yet how to say
    those acrobatics
        aren't meant

to jollify the day. He's
    hungry, poking
        away at nothing

for crumbs we failed to bring: how to tell her?

IX

Ducks lie close together
    in morning dew, wary-eyed,
        bills pointing at the pond:

roused by squirrels,
    those early risers,
        air's a-whir with wings.

Sad to think of leaving
        this place. A helicopter
                with mysterious purpose

appears above the trees,
        moving low. Its circles
                tightening,

the ducks cling to the pondedge, right to fear.

The Edge

Living that year at the edge
of the ravine,
sloped down to the woods, we listened

to the animals before the town
awoke, blurring
the limits of our days,

forcing its round, the needs
of others.
Near sleep, after loving, we felt

part of a stillness with the dark
and all its creatures,
holding to the edge of where we lived.

For Helen

You chip a tooth, complain
of getting old.
Well, I've felt old for years.

"You're as old
as you are,"
I quip and parry frowns.

"Look, we're in this
together"—that
never fails, you're in

my arms and young. Warmth
to warmth, we're
bound to last forever.

Map

I unfold it on the desk
to trace you once again.
Though cut off by a smudge

of mountains, ropes
of water stretched between,
how easily I spread a hand

across the space that separates.
                    But this
cramped sheet, while true,

does not tell all. What of
that span no map will ever
show, sharper for being unseen?

The Writer's Wife

Deep in your northwood's fastness,
snowbound half the year, you complain,

he tells me, of problems with the stove,
dirt, loneliness, yet says he's proud

of your tenacity, your faith in him.
Meanwhile he writes what only you will read.

No one else would do this for him,
he whose work has come to nothing.

Amputee

Something kept the blood from
going round—
he gave up one leg like a prize,

and then the other. Soon it would
be his arms.
He called it an "unwilling heart."

Jollying nurses, once he rocked
the ward with—
"Who's for football?" from his bedpan throne.

When he was readied for the saw again,
we wished him
well. He waved his bandaged hand:

"Now you see it, now you don't,"
he quipped. They
told us he died laughing under gas.

Boston

South Station, very early, and
come to read midwestern poems
at Tufts, due in an hour, seedy

in my all-night-slept-in suit,
I need a shave. The john of Savarin's
is full. I try the public one.

A bum is scraping skin off
at the mirror. I stand behind him,
fumble for the switch, lift

my cordless shaver to the jaw.
The tatooed stripper on his arm
begins to bump. Soap drips bloody

from his straightedge. "Give it here,"
he mutters. Razor plowing down,
I know he means it, hand

it to him, juice full on,
grab my suitcase, then half shaved
move off to read those poems.

The Exchange

As I turned from the bar,
my back to him,
he beat it through the door
with every cent I had.

"Happens everyday," the barkeep
said. I burned for weeks,
imagined trapping him
in alleyways, fists ready.

Then his face lost focus,
I found myself remembering
the tip he gave me
on a horse, his winning manner

and his guts. I'd learned
at some expense
a truth about myself,
and was twice robbed.

The Loser

He's there outside again, holding up
the tavern wall, whatever the day.

Never completely under—cadging,
wheedling through his tale. Few seem

to pity him. Others remember the girl
who ditched him for a carnival,

and promised she'd be back. So his
long wait began. Well, someone had to hurt,

and he was chosen: town drunk, town loser,
plastered with the ads against the wall.

Clown

Brush in hand, blinking
    under
        a sombrero of whitewash,

he's shoved feetfirst
    into
        the cannon's mouth.

Drum pointing in their chests
    children
        hold their ears.

It's no surprise to them
    that,
        blast still ringing,

he hits the net and springs up
    bloodless,
        on his toes.

The Last Romantic

"Le Duc" we hailed him to his pinched
Napoleonic face, behind
the frail brushed back, "Le Fou."

All day he'd prowl the boulevards,
gilt cane ticking, for Insult,
and when he found it, up went cane

and swish! another passer-by'd
be sliced and stacked like sausage
on the dark shelf of his mind.

Thus Le Due until that chilly
afternoon at Jean's Cafe.
There he perched, like a hawk, for

Slight. The tourist hardly stopped
to gawk inside: more than enough.
"Crapaud!" Le Duc arose and charged—

what a shattering of pride!
Before they shrove him of Jean's
windowglass, Le poor Fou died.

To Roger Blin

My shaky French, my coarse
Bohemian ways,
must have amused you—

you who had the "mark,"
the fiery
haunted look of postwar Paris.

Sweating over poems
in a drab
leftbank hotel, I fantasized

your life, slowly to feel
as you directed
Lorca's plays, myself

upon that stage. Was it
a style, warm
and yet severe, an honesty?

Now opening Genet's *Letters
to Roger Blin,*
I feel ashamed. I asked

too much of you: a path,
a way, the art
to make life possible.

Dean Dixon, Welcome Home

Weary of their praise—"those
black expressive hands,"
tired of saying Brahms

not Gershwin was your man,
you left behind do-gooders
and their scented wives,

sailed from their "Negro Firsts"
to prove you had the gift.
Now, tall before the orchestra,

drawing urgent chords, you raise
those hands again. Times
are changed, they say, and someone

needs what you alone can give.
Seasons late, you're
welcomed home, Dean Dixon, friend.

Busker

Facing the playhouse queue,
straining through songs

all can remember, she muffs
a high note at the end.

As we start to shuffle in,
she scrambles for the loot.

Fat, seedy—never mind—
she is so purely what she is

no actor could do more.
Leaving the queue, I follow

her all night, hands full of coins,
songs ringing everywhere.

Church Concert (London)

Juan Arrau, guitarist, your Frescobaldi,
    Albeniz,
stir the crowded aisles of Saint Martin's,

warm the shivering woman, feet tapping
    on the pew,
and the man dozing against a pillar looks

wildly where the stained glass shatters in
    the priest's eyes.
You pierce them with a deep song from your

native South—the rush of sea, waves like
    horns against
a wall. The audience set free, Trafalgar Square

will never be the same—Nelson like
    a prowhead,
adrift once more upon the Spanish Main.

Keats House

I sign the guest book
where some wit scrawled—
"Keats had a sore Fanny!"

Move by books, portraits,
manuscripts, his chair.
Sad—I get the feel of him,

yet something's gone,
whatever made him write:
the girl, a nightingale,

seasons of mist, which had
their music too? Beyond
the house the Heath's

not as it was, yet cold enough
to raise that chill which
kept him in these rooms, a poet

and a dying man, to do the work.

At Shakespeare's Tomb

Tickets trailing from their fists, whispering
    about the need
      to patch, renew,
the priests take our money, lead us where

you lie boxed in beneath your likeness.
    Outside the Avon
      active with
detergent, crested here and there by dizzy swans.

Along the banks your worshippers vision you
    wading, fishing,
      rushing past them
with a mate, poached deer on shouldered pole.

Naughty, you charm them, as in the playhouse
    down the river
      you'll amaze.
In spite of Lear you have become an industry:

ten fleets of bus, fifteen Chinese cooks,
    five Italian,
      a pox of
Ye Olde this and that, guides in your father's

and your daughter's houses—possibly
    your trundle bed,
      likely your
chamberpot. Tourists, cameras weighing

down their heads, seize you at last. Meanwhile
    a grateful bed-
    and-breakfast town
rejoices in your power, its poetry.

Sniper

An inch to the left
and I'd be twenty years
of dust by now. I can't

walk under trees without
his muzzle tracks me.
He'd hit through branches,

leaves pinned to his shoulders
whistling. We searched him
everywhere—up trunks,

in caves, down pits. Then
one night, his island taken,
he stepped from jungle

shade, leaves still pinned
upon him glistening
in the projector's light,

and tiptoed round to watch
our show, a weary kid
strayed in from trick-or-treat.

Forward Observers

Our lensed hill-splitting eyes
useless in the dark, they
flanked us through the night.

Indispensable, we called
down thunder from the hills,
and saved a thousand.

Each of us worth, some claimed,
one hundred men,
they needed yet despised us.

Their bodies held like sandbags.
We survived,
part of something coming, vile as war.

Thoroughbred Country

Lexington to Louisville: the Greyhound
moves through bluegrass, the stud, its mares,
caught delicately on the soft hill.

It's all horse talk past Calumet,
"richest acres" in the world.
Blue—the grass, the sky, the blood.

Conscripts in the bus, straight
from the hollows, first time away,
are wondering what awaits them.

A black horse gallops from the shadows.
The young men look away.
No one speaks until we enter Louisville.

Evening

Weary, I seek relief behind
the paper, before the set
where they emerge, the victims,

through walls and floorboards,
summoning to a ritual
hung with fear, myself enacted,

inflicting and inflicted pain.
From fissures in the earth,
from smoking thatch they rush

toward me, arms like torches,
children grasped between,
cries hurtling oceans meant

to separate. What can I do?
Put down, switch off—
plunge to the barricades of sleep.

Sunday. The Bells.

All over town they
rise from beds,
heavy with dreams
of sons dying in Viet Nam.

Sunday. The bells ring
in the terrible emptiness
of bedrooms their distant
sons dream girls into.

Letter to Jean-Paul Baudot, at Christmas

Friend, on this sunny day, snow sparkling
everywhere, I think of you once more,
how many years ago, a child Resistance

fighter trapped by Nazis in a cave
with fifteen others, left to die, you became
a cannibal. Saved by Americans,

the taste of a dead comrade's flesh foul
in your mouth, you fell onto the snow
of the Haute Savoie and gorged to purge yourself,

somehow to start again. Each winter since
you were reminded, vomiting for days.
Each winter since you told me at the Mabillon,

I see you on the first snow of the year
spreadeagled, face buried in that stench.
I write once more, Jean-Paul, though you don't

answer, because I must: today men do far worse.
Yours in hope of peace, for all of us,
before the coming of another snow.

From *Selected Poems* (1976)

The Face

Weekly at the start
of the documentary
on World War II

a boy's face, doomed,
sharply beautiful,
floats in the screen,

a dark balloon
above a field of barbs,
the stench of gas.

Whoever holds the
string
will not let go.

Rain

Lazy afternoon, rain
drizzling down the path,
soft hum of my daughter

and her friends: moments
of quiet, untroubling.
But now the neighbor's child

skips out in old boots,
umbrella arched, rain
sopping her blue dress.

Like a small animal
she caves against the storm:
yesterday her father caught

messing with the sitter,
today the hurried packing,
and the constant rain.

Sirens

Someone calls for help,
always.
He called yesterday,

he will call tomorrow.
Yesterday he was on fire,
today his hand

was chewed off by the steel
teeth of a combine,
tomorrow he will lurch

from a smashed car,
take two steps, collapse
onto his red shadow.

His voice, familiar,
pierces everywhere:
it will be heard.

The Gorge

There is something
between us
I must pass to
reach you,
hand over hand,
legs swinging,
sharp scent
of brush rising
from the gorge bed.

My arms strain
as finally
I sight you—
you
who are most

aware of the
painful art
I practice,
and for whom.

Ox

Another day
    half over,
raising hoofs
    where horns
slice through
    the clouds.
Darkness
    streams down
the flanks,
    filling the
scented field,
    but somewhere
night is
    touched off
by a horn,
    columns of
light form
    under the
rippling body—
    once more
to pasture
    in my eyes.

Mole

Hunched in the basement,
shadow on the wall,
six feet down and glad to be alive.

Overhead, wilting memory
of long dog days,
earthmovers rumble in the haze

through trees, corn, soybeans—
steel, concrete,
glass to come. I need

this burrow, cool, sunken
with roots. What
will remain, I wonder, when

I tunnel up from where I hunch,
shadow on the wall,
six feet down and glad to be alive.

I. M. Pablo Picasso

(for my father)

All is ordinary again—
in a thousand places,
convergences,

displaced parts flying
together: an ear,
a nose, a breast spinning

like a hand-grenade,
a third eye shot
with cloud, deep, staring,

and here, in Chicago
a great
flapping of wings.

Carlo Crivelli: Crucifixion

Sulphurous storm-
light
over Calvary.

The Sold Man
yellowing
under thorns,

feet caked with
stations
of the cross.

Soon a blossoming
from
the cairn:

those hooded
stones
will split.

Snow

Centuries
snow
has drifted
"feather like"
through poems,
so thick,
one on a ladder,
connoisseur
of snows,
archivist
of weathers,
gingerly raising
a ten-foot pen,
climbing
after it onto

that frozen waste,
would find
much snow,
little poetry.
Meanwhile
the writer,
after many weeks,
feels
his hand move—
now it stops,
a footprint artist
pausing in the snow.

The Goose

Magnificent
against October maples
the goose
twisting in downdraft
shot to the highway,
crushed on my wheels—
I braked
wanting to rush out,
imagined
its strong arc south again.

Blaring cars
shadowed
as I started up,
driving for miles
in innocence
in guilt
not caring where I headed,
a whiteness
mangled
in the maples, everywhere.

Love Poem

Startle my wife again—
"Where will we lay our bones?"

Harmless, you'd think, yet
she's berserk. "Mere joshing,"

I protest. She will not
listen. I want an island

for us, apart, ringed with stones,
clusterings of flowers

merging us closer through
the all of time. She thinks

me mad with dreaming,
but it's love for her

which spurs me, this need
to know we'll never separate.

Friendship

He writes again. Since his divorce
a fist has never left his chest.

He needs my words, and so I fill
a sheet—what joy it gives

to utter words to eyes that plead
from paper. I place the softest

on his cheek, his brow, a special one
upon his mouth. Sigh across

the page that he still has a friend.
Now off to do its loving work,

my scroll of bandages and kisses,
my dried and flattened heart.

Barbecue

Mister and Missus
Carnalot,
friendly folk,
stoke up the fire.

His and Hers aprons
flush in the
char-smoke. They
are ablaze while

the spit turns,
rekindling ashes,
sipping, seasoning,
done to a turn.

Readying long forks,
prongs move together,
his toward Hers,
hers toward His.

Shadow

Always coming, neat head
tilted, "Mad" Nolgate
shadows these streets for years,

surviving playground taunts,
the school's Least Likely.
Prompt as the townclock,

passes old classmates
at work, flusters wives
wilting by chain-store greens,

scattering their kids—
thunder on pavement,
storming through grass.

Let loose inside himself,
cushioned in air,
he walks on forever.

Rites of Passage

Indian river swollen brown and swift:
the pebble from my hand sounds above
     the southfield—

soybeans, corn, cicadas. Stone rings
touch the bank, ripple up my arm.
     In the grass

a worm twists in webbed air (how things
absorb each other)—on a branch
     a sparrow

tenses, gray. As grass stirs it bursts
from leaves, devouring. I close my book.
     With so much

doing everywhere, words swimming green,
why read? I see and taste silence.
     Starlings flit,

blue/black feathers raising spume
of dandelions, young fluttering
     in the twigs.

I think of my grown son who runs
and heaves me to my feet—our
     promised walk

through woods. As he pulls back a branch
hair on his forearm glistens
     like the leaves

we brush by. I follow down the path
we've loved for years. We try to
     lose ourselves,

yet there's the river, churning south.
I muse on what I've given,
     all I can't.

My son moves toward the bank, then turns.
I stop myself from grasping
     at his hand.

From *Collected Poems 1953–1983* (1984)

Cherries

Because I sit eating cherries
which I did not pick
a girl goes bad under

the elevator tracks, will
never be whole again.
Because I want the full bag,

grasping, twenty-five children
cry for food. Gorging,
I've none to offer. I want

to care, I mean to, but not
yet, a dozen cherries
rattling at the bottom of my bag.

One by one I lift them to
my mouth, slowly break
their skin—twelve nations

bleed. Because I love, because
I need cherries, I
cannot help them. My happiness,

bought cheap, must last forever.

Elm

Beetles smaller than
rice-grains hollowed
the weathered trunk,

piling sawdust high.
Fearing another storm
might axe the sparse-

leafed branches through
the shingles, I loosed
bird-feeder ropes, gave

up the elm to Shabbona
Tree Service. Watched
birds spiral, squirrels

bolt as limbs crashed
down. By afternoon, sun
warmed the jagged stump,

and the stone roof once
overhung by leaves. Season
turning, frost spiked

the twigless air. Soon
snow filled emptiness
between the shrubs. I

fed my elm-logs to the
fire, sending ghost-
blossoms to the sky.

Savants

Their hour had come
and gone: notions
blueprinted, years

of infinite zeros,
halved, quartered,
atomed for this day—

test-tubes of dust
measured to shake the
world. Now it was

done. Reaming traces
from their nails,
scattering like rocks

they'd blasted from
the earth, they turned
to raking gardens,

lecturing on peace,
regrets black-signatured
across an ashen page.

Secret codes unlearnt,
they crawled back to the
past on hands and knees.

In Our Time

When after the blast
they turned to the poet,
he asked for a handful
of nails. Pounded them
like phrases into old
boards. No bittersweet,
no roses now. He knelt
in silence in the wasted
town—a stain under the
fallout moon. Nails, line
by line, his only song.

Where We Are

I sit beneath the linden's
heart-spread leaves, watch

three starlings on the bird-
bath watching me. Book on

one knee, I drain my glass:
young shoots, already doomed,

thrust withering tendrils
through the clay-bogged soil.

Last night, at the May Fair,
girls in Elizabethan garb

offered a madrigal to buds
of spring. Today the neighbor's

cat stalks fledglings in the
pine. Time was I'd run him

off. Now I just sit and trust
to his bad luck. Slowly sun

tinges leaves, hazes pine
needles. A mower sputters—

cat leaps from the shade,
into the moment, where we are.

The Ordinary

To love the ordinary—
fifty feet of dandelions
    and burdock,

and a small house perched
on concrete under a dying
    Chinese elm.

To be content with neighbor-
banter over a crooked fence,
    days, nights, years.

And not to regret—sun
torching the willow-oak—
    some Elsewhere.

Dirge

Hair, weathered
nest, shedding

from nerve ends.
Ears, nose, mouth:

muting, knobbing,
pursing into caverns

where necessities—
air, water, pottage—

filter, slop. As
eyes blur, worlds

move further from
the flushed beast—

heart—pounding
its sullen song.

I. M. Eugenio Montale

The day you turned to face
the nothingness men fear—

drunken with your secret,
like the eel, "sister of

the rainbow," arcing through
seven seas—was like

any other. Poet, you needed
fear, as one needs salt

to feel the deepest wounds.
This morning, in a Milan

hospital's antiseptic chill,
you turned for the last time

to meet that void, words
drowned in waves of light.

Dawn

Five a.m., and I've been
up for hours. My lamp,
false star, holds back

the dark. In the next
room my wife guards our
closeness deep in dream.

I love this sleeplessness,
cloistered unbroken
hours over a spotless page,

the book with all the
answers on the shelf. I
doodle on one, thumb

through the other, now
and then. This hour, it
makes no difference.

I sit back, let thoughts
come as they may. Who
knows, before dawn rides

the oak across the way,
the book may jostle just a
bit, the paper bear a poem.

November

First frost, the blue spruce
against my window's shagged,
and the sky is sombering. I

draw close to the fire, inward
with all that breathes. This
morning, stacking firewood,

I shattered leaf-drifts by
the shed, trailing the rabbit
burrowed there. Soon we'll

be wintering, he and I, our
paths will often cross upon
the snow. I drink good

luck to both of us, he in his
sticks and leaves, and I
in mine. Summer, the neighbor

blamed his marauding for the
shrinking salad patch, hinting
the yards would be well rid

of something two dogs, even
a tent of wire could not keep
out. I muttered to myself,

dropped my carrot like a
calling card behind the shed.
Now the spruce twists slowly

into dark. I pour another
drink. Within the hour the moon
will kindle every frosted limb.

You Must Change Your Life

Of all things one might be:
a squirrel lopes by

busy at being himself
in a tough nutless world,

cats at his young, rain
slanting in his nest,

night falling, winter
not provided for—

no questions to ask
of himself or anyone.

Why I Write

Someone years ago forced
me to learn the alphabet,
spell, form sentences
of mouth, of hand—
long streets which, on

occasion, led to resonant
spots: at one I surprised
a bluejay bickering in
a pinetree—that blue/green
flash carried me to the

next sentence, at the end
of which two lovers came
to a full stop. Thus grew
my habit: paragraphs of
wheezy cats, windbagging

crickets, children whooping
under bell-clear skies.
These days I stroll along,

casually turn corners where
someone in black collects

my lines on a white page,
then scurries off, long
scroll trailing. No idea
what he does with them.
The other day, in a small

town, on an odd shelf, I
glimpsed a book bearing
my name. Tempted to look
inside, I hurried on. I'm
really too faint-hearted.

Desk

Dictionary
Typewriter

Paper
Seven pipes

Ashtray
Three pens

Two elbows

Nomads

(Meshed, Iran)

Yearly they descend
scorched slopes, scatter
black tents between
abandoned wells, to graze
flocks where children
tumble in the dust.

Indifferent to strangers
come to stare, shying
from their smells. Evenings,
draped in matted skins
knotted with sheep-gut,
they squat before tents,
smoke, laugh, bend above
flutes. Their women,
turning sheep-spits, recall
days of drought, when
foraging on all fours,
they scratched for tufts
with the herds. Chanting
to flute-notes, they turn turn,
far from the lives of
strangers—soft, up on
hind legs, coming, going.

The Great Exception

After the inspection at the Gate
she joined the others waiting
in blue shapeless gowns for their

assignment. From the start she
felt it a mistake, but what she'd
heard here of the other place

discouraged her complaining. Silent
gazes disapproved. Maybe it was
an air acquired on the streets,

a painted scarlet letter. Alone
as always, she trailed behind
the others: reaching at last

The Spirit of the Universe, learned
to her astonishment she was the
Great Exception, chosen as an image

of her kind. She wondered what
was expected of such favor, found
it was in Heaven's interest to token

fairness—all were equal here.
Yet where was compensation in this
Paradise of inner gardens, secured

from men? Pining away a dozen years
of everlasting life, she must
revolt. Her tongue, long gentled,

found its former salt. Loosening
her gown, unpinning her hair, she
was discovered wandering naked in

archangels' quarters. For that
and other sins she was advanced,
with proclamation, to a higher

order, greatest of Great Exceptions.

Exterminator

Phone vibrates all winter. The
exterminator cringes—
yet another squeal, demanding

he come fast. He plays at cat
and mouse, stalling them hours,
days. Then pocketing thick

gloves, flashlight, steelwool,
poison he enters musty corners,
sets dry traps, pours tempting

pellets into little paper boats,
launches them here and there.
As he stuffs holes, he contemplates

the toughness of a world which
outlaws creatures he has learned
to love: starved from frozen

corn-stripped fields, small wonder
they outsmart those who grudge them
a few crumbs, a little warmth. The

exterminator does his job, takes his
money, leaves. In the long run of
things, he knows who will survive.

The City: A Cycle

I. Calendar

Another year: curbs
strewn with Christmas
trees, tinsel floats

the thaw. We've stumbled
to the end, driven by
storms still rumbling

overhead. Earth speaks
what we already know,
in pain relearn. On

the wall the Japanese
calendar, pure of our
devisings, mists beyond

peaks, temples, pines
where we survive. Page
by page guards secrets,

as we start out again.

II. *Grant Park*

Crush of frost:
they walk sharp-eyed
the paths familiar
as their floors—

men nearing death,
our fathers, pulled
unresisting to
the center. There,

on charged corners,
they watch, chat,
doze, heads lifted
to the wind, that

bringer, taker away—
music in the welter
of their lives. Day
deepens. They rouse

from benches, shiver,
stare about, then
cautiously return.
Each to his place,

to read once more
of what the day has
brought: another
birth, another death.

III. *Downtown*

He is the one their laws
are made for—
speeder drunkard despoiler

of daughters. Born for
tar and feathers, he stalks
in shadow. In shops his

is the dollar held up to
the light. Threatened
by factory whistles, slying

from work, he's first for
welfare. Nightly thanks city-
hall with chalked graffiti:

mayor policechief judge.

IV. Lake Dawn

Slow spread of light
beyond the tracks,
fingering bare branches

of the oak. After
thick year on year
another chance to find

what dawn, rising on
frosty air, will
bring. Yesterday, ice

floes on the lake, a
revelation: nothing's
warmer than sun-webbed

snow, boots scorching
on the crust. What
will I learn today?

I thirsted seasons,
dragging a leaden shadow
into nothingness. Now,

as fire meets ice, I see.

V. City Spring

There's a slow
twisting underground,
as if a giant,

winter long buried
under ice,
clutching roots,

now turns face-up,
stirring the
ancient sexual play:

everywhere his warm
flesh touches—
green, yellow, red.

VI. The Beach

Winds over the city,
where once, fanned by

bird-wings, we strolled
the lake-edge. Now

cars and factories fume
every breathing thing,

blacken trees, speckle
flowers, blight grass,

fill lungs of children
leapfrogging on the

sand. They stop their play
to wonder as, fins spread,

mouths agape, dead alewives
float in with the tide.

VII. Monarchs

A shower of spotted
wings, monarchs drift
by factory gates,
settling in trees.

Steel beats for miles.
How fresh, early autumn
gusts that teeter
branches as they cling.

Easy to mistake them,
clustered in the pine,
for blazing cones. Thus
they outwit the starlings

wheeling by. Lassitude,
soft giving up, has
stilled their wings,
summer folds behind them.

VIII. Winter Storm

Bitter night. The westwind
blasts us from our moorings.
Beyond, sends towns like drunken
boats over five hundred miles

of frozen fields. Sirens, which
all night foretold, the radio
which echoed, whimpering, have
given up, and now the city is

the wind's. We're left to our
devices. Fifteen below, the
storm has just begun. A
sputtering gas-jet, shrinking

candle keep us from perishing,
as we watch through whirled
trees a sky scorched with stars.
Sleepless, we pace room to room,

waiting the dawn. Know there
are those for whom dawn never
came, worlds that storms wiped
out before, and storms to come.

IX. Chicago Christmas

Midday, watch the stranger
inching down the icy street. Last
night we opened presents by
the fire, ate, drank one toast
after another. Flames crackled,

reeled with our contentment.
Now we return to selves, peace
settling like ash. Grab my
duffle, head down to the lake,
tramp snow, knee-high, across

the bridge, air stinging nose
and eyes. Soon ice will melt.
Somewhere this water flows
tides will batter shores where
hunger's in the wind. Tomorrow

left-overs of feasts will drip
from garbage trucks, tinseled
trees strew curbs of houses
street on street, and wonderment
of pampered children dim. As

sun dips behind glazed rooftops,
imagine scrawling across twilight—
"Live as if this day will never
end." Recross the bridge,
back to whatever's left of joy.

There Are Days

Days when speech won't come,
there's pain in words.

To utter nothings:
it's raining, there's the sun.

Not caring less but more,
how hard the language

of consent. It's in
the deeps of silence,

hour on hour, I feel
grains, stones, trace

names of all I lack.
Then suddenly

hear train whistles,
possibilities,

return, surprised, to
fragments of myself.

The Word

How inadequate words are
to all we know and feel—

Love Justice Honor Truth—
each emptier than the other.

If there were one word, not
spun of cloud but struck

from stone, a sudden cry,
brief, mighty, to show us as

we really are, small, cruel,
it would to our amazement

gather, merge into a final
tongue, echoing years—

the silence that would follow
prepare us for the world.

Soul

Often evoked, exalted,
the soul might crouch
for years between

breastbone, esophagus,
conscience in a cage,
buzzing the ears,

pulling firm strings
behind eyes, patching up
heart-sores with cloudy

visions. My soul just
sits here, out of
action, arms wrapped

around stiffening knees,
sour looks on its
once friendly face.

I resent its power,
the scorn for all I write—
wrung from dreams it

feeds me, now and then.

Ellwood House

The carriage-way, bristling beneath
gimcrack, sends thorniest vibrations
from the house that barbs built. From
here came deft contraptions, honed

steel for cattle flanks, blocking
the cowboy's path, cutting antelope
from the most fragrant grass. The wire
piled high, each barb a dollar in

the bank. Prize objects gathered:
lacquer from the East, marble from Italy,
commode with spindly legs from France,
carved swan-cradle that rocked sons

of czars, bannister spiraling like an
oaken fence in the cathedral hall. While
the town gaped, others claimed the idea,
set up new plants. More coils rolled

out, parceling prairie miles, the West,
on through the world. They prospered:
children schooled expensively, women
scented, jeweled, gowned to divert

rich and famous. Two strands of twisted
wire cleared a cornfield for a mansion
like a sugared cake, set among weathered
silos. Enticed great chefs from Europe,

fashioned a ballroom where chanteuses,
chamber music thrilled the night.
Through war, peace, slavery, revolt
their fiddlers led the dance—

parting man from man, beast from beast.

Waking Up in Streator

I am wakened by a poem
I have never heard, in

a town never visited
deep in Illinois. Last

night, due to read poems
500 miles away—now

shaggy from dream—I
remember a friend, long dead,

who grew up in Streator,
played football, talked tough,

scorning all dreamers.
Yet one night, late,

loosened by beer, confessed
he'd once written a poem.

Constellation

Behind the super-
market where we
forage for our

lives, beyond the
parking lot, crammed
garbage bins—

thick heads of
bee-swarmed
seed-choked

sunflowers blaze
down on me through
fogged noon air.

Nodding

Half way through the play—
Marlowe at that—
I nod off into five acts

of my own, become Edward II,
betrayed, restored, betrayed
again. Wavering, frivolous,

tossed by intrigues, I snore
away, indifferent to rumors
ravaging my throne. Dream

scene on scene, cringe as they
butcher one friend, then
another. Hunger for innocence,

whimper for peace, damn my
adulterous queen, luring
assassins to me. The book

slips from my fingers, spins
like a crown. Startled,
I rise—the play has ended.

Siberia

Small wood towns silvered
        by birches,
sharp blue at windows, doors.

Grimed, forgotten domes,
        a gold cross:
cows, chickens haunt the tombs.

Train lurches on: ten miles west
        of Irkutsk,
where Chekhov, bound for convict

Sakhalin, once spent a night,
        I hear three
sisters longing, Moscow, Moscow!

At the Siberian heart, concrete
        crammed with facts:
who produced what, how much, when,

in what spirit. On the
        last ruled sheet
a finger-smudge points like

a holy candle. November: in
        seven days
drums, bugles, flags will whip

town after town. On wind-
        scourged platforms
throngs mill under likenesses

of hero farmers—ribboned,
        bemedaled,
exalted by a fourth sister,

one Chekhov did not know, who
        pitying
her sisters' discontent accepted

solitude and hardship, despite
        the need, at
times unbearable, of Moscow, Moscow!

Juggler

Someone with skill juggles
three worlds together,
rainbow, miraculous arc.

Something compels a fourth,
widening the circle. Five,
six float in the charged

steep of his mind: soon
others whirl his wrist.
Seven, eight—now he's on

his toes, up, up, rising
with the music of the
spheres. Still unsatisfied,

risks the lot, down on his
knees. He dare not drop one.
Our lives depend on it.

Exile's Return

I've decided to return,
to show them. Any place,
too long, begins to grate.

On coming to this island,
I was treated like a
lord. As one might expect,

familiar now, I disappoint,
my image pales. Daubing
a sunset on the Western Cliff,

I hear them jeer. Turn,
catch them gawking at
my canvas. Drape the easel

with my smock, enter my hut,
refuse their dole of food.
For that my woman will not

come. First time in months,
I sleep alone. Waken
to stench outside my door—

a dead dog's rotting there.
Later, I'll pack my paints,
my few mildewed belongings,

hop the mailboat to the harbor,
make for home. Humbled,
perhaps, but far from done.

My soul is what they're after.
I'll show those ingrates up
for what they are. Brush

dipped in blood, I'll paint
a masterpiece none dare ignore.
My art will make them suffer.

Smoke

Smoke from my briar
hovers between pages
    on my lap,

clouds thought on
thought, drifts toward
    voices in

dark suits newsmongering
another day. I
    choke the sound,

knock ashes out, tamp
fresh leaf in, light
    up again.

"Smoke!" my grandson
cries, climbing beside
    me, joyfully

grasping rings. A
moment, shielded there,
    I hold him

to me, soothing the
outrage in the hot bowl
    of my mind.

Watching War Movies

Always the same: watching
World War II movies on TV,
landing barges bursting onto

islands, my skin crawls—
heat, dust—the scorpion
bites again. How I deceived

myself. Certain my role would
not make me killer, my unarmed
body called down fire from

scarred hills. As life took
life, blood coursed into
one stream. I knew one day,

the madness stopped, I'd make
my pilgrimage to temples,
gardens, serene masters of

a Way which pain was bonding.
Atoms fuse, a mushroom cloud,
the movie ends. But I still

stumble under camouflage, near
books of tranquil Buddhas by the
screen. The war goes on and on.

Memorial Day

Three deliberate shots
fire this quiet town,

scatter sparrows from
the willow-oak, touch

the scar where over thirty
years ago the mortar

fragment hit: I know
once more how good it is

to live. Thinking of the
boy struck down beside

me by that shell, I see
him sink into slow jungle

green, shock burned forever
in his eyes. Again I

crawl to comfort his last
breath. Even now there's

nothing I can do but, as
the bugle fades, remember.

Choral

Goodby, philosophers,
sorry we didn't listen:

now we pay. You
reasoned moderation,

we chose excess.
Extolled effort, we

lazed unconcerned.
Praised wisdom,

as we scratched behinds
and yawned. Not giving

up, you warned of
barbarism, as we goose-

stepped off. Railed
at gods, who shoved us,

eyes closed, to our
knees. Did you mean

to leave us, bungling,
half alive in a world

half made, stirring
a fission-caldron?

How will we ever know?
Your tomes are laced

with worms, your statues
molder, faceless,

in abandoned squares.

Machines

Centuries
before reckoning,
cave walls,

stone-scratched
with birdwings,
took flight—

hurling with
flint arrows
down the black

hole of time.
Fracturing worlds,
brief puffs

of dust, metal
and bone.
Yesterday—two

planes colliding,
five hundred
wiped out.

Grief

Our first home, after journeying
years. Look up from my desk
through maples, spruce, sycamore

at sunrise, dusk, wonder that
this place is ours. Through
sun-fired boughs, I watch a young

man amble, zipping hunting jacket,
from the house across the way,
toss shotgun in the back seat

of his Dodge, rev up the motor,
race off for deerblood. Tonight
he lies in the funeral parlor,

lost to cries of grief. Strangers,
we visit mourners in the room
he paneled, stare in the mirror

he framed and polished to a blaze.
Confused, they wonder whose words
sent him frenzied into night to drink

with hunting buddies. Out of their
pain we trace long months of failure:
divorced father of two, returned

to them jobless, rented house
gone up in flames. Clasping our
hands, their eyes demand reasons.

We offer pity, return to our home,
shadowed by trees, ashamed we can
offer no more, for the death of a son.

The Rose

My love, as I lie next
to you, close against your
        pain, I begin

to understand the secret
of the rose, how always
        beneath one

petal another forms, how
none of its fragrant
        lips reveal

this joining. Thirty years
I've tried to know what holds
        me to you.

Now: deep within, beyond
what hand or eye can reach,
        the thorn

is bared against the
first impulsive thrust,
        against the last.

Classroom

Achievements of T'ang
Dynasty poets pass
over the blonde girl

in the striped dress,
third row on the left.
Wretchedly, she bends

over a letter—life
overwhelms. In or
out of love, she's on

that heaviest of seas.
Wang Wei's vision fills
the room. My chalky

mutterings of mountains,
rushing winds stir
nothing in her eyes. Her

thoughts are dynasties
away, shadowed by all
her life need ever know.

Evelyn

When she phones late, I listen
for disaster. At times
the epilogues were left to me.

She vows to end her life: I
grasp the phone, shaking as
the line goes dead, fearing

the worst until she calls again.
At times I've told her firmly— "No.
No use to visit, you need help

more than consolation." That
always hurts. As teacher I listened
hours, pitied. Now she sees me

father that she never knew. Last
night she was more easy, back with
a boy who hasn't torched a building

in some time. Touched by common
need, they soothe each other in
their wretchedness. Reminded of

her gifts, of comfort in reordering
one's world, she made me guardian
of all her tortured art, so with

her end I might restore another.
It's when she probes my poems, seeking
answers to unmake her wrongs, I

most despair. She chides me when my
lines don't pacify, presses me to
change them for her sake and mine.

Recently I've fathomed, phone gripped
hard, she thinks that I'm the one
needs help. She's there to give it.

The Park

All summer long rednecks,
high-school dropouts rev
motorbikes and souped-up
cars across the isle of
grass, jeer at cops cruising
as the horseshoes fly.
Strollers, joggers, children
traipsing to the city pool
flinch at hoots and whistles,
radio blasts recoiling from
the trees. Autumn, as leaves

ambered over picnickers
carousing on their patch, three—
caught upending gravestones
in the cemetery close by—
said they'd no place to go
but call upon the dead.
Winter sifts still white hours.
The toughs, the dropouts,
holed up somewhere with their
beer and joints, dream of
horseshoes looping shadowy oaks.

Firewood

The old Norwegian backs his pick-up
on the grass, helps stack oak
and maple, split clean for my winter
hours. As we stir a rabbit, he

tells of tramping through woods on
this very land some thirty years
before. Points, squinting, two hundred
yards toward the river, talks fast

for a farmer, amused at my pure pleasure
at the wood we pile together on the
lawn, this sharp December day. Last
log in place, he lights a cigarette,

puffs deep, muses, "Never got back
to the old country." Say I'm sorry,
speak of fjords flaming under midnight
suns. He shrugs, spits at a tree,

reasons, "Where else in the world
could I say, president's a friend of
mine?" He motions west. "When we
were boys in Dixon he went down the

cattle market with me and the old man—
had good times." "Must feel proud,"
I tell him. He asks me what I do.
Confess I teach, write poems. He

eyes me warily, climbs into his cab,
starts the motor, rolls the window down,
asks, "Did you vote for him?" I
shake my head, wave as he roars off.

I tidy around the woodpile, haul in
some logs, light up our first fire in
our first real home, sit back, relax.
Just as he said, the seasoned flames

lick high into the draft, the logs
burn slow. In spite of politics, this
is an honest deal. I'll have to make
it last. He might not come again.

Old Folks Home

Always near dusk
in the shadow of
cedars, he mourns
the loss of another

day. The empty path
winds to fields pulsing
gold, green under
vapors, rain-fresh

furrows stretching
miles. Each afternoon
the old man ambles
under branches,

remembering his farm,
wife long dead, sons
buried in lives
of their own. There

he stands hours, keen
to the cool scent
of fullness—now
without purpose where

corn-tassels blow.
Returns to the bare
room, high above cedars,
gathering gold and green.

Fortune Teller

In half-light, over a cloudy ball,
mumbo-jumboing what you crave,

I, diviner of palms, trace
life, love, profit, await your

silver. Lift one hand, the other,
wonder which clamped in greed,

stole from the needy, turned down
the thumb that might have saved.

Such innocents here. Follow each
crease, trying to please, name

lines, wrinkles, seams. Whisper
the future, over and over, pretending

to find in your hand what is there
in your eyes—await your silver.

Flesh

Skin's blotched, all
night I've scratched.
Arm's become a scroll,
a deep stigmata.

Message from within:
something's giving up,
hardly worth the candle
anymore. Under my

scholar's cap, read
doom. Spread ointment
as the hooks etch
crimson. Knock back

a glass of wine, hoping
for ease. Is this
how it all ends? Eyes
dim, breath short, skin

festering? Again the
tingling, everywhere
at once. Today,
tomorrow—bear up,

best I can, to the
unbearable. Swig my
wine, slide down its
shaky rope to peace.

Cosmos

Moon, magnified 1000
times, overwhelms—

hunched on this crumb
of earth, I cringe as

tongues sum up existence
for me. Out there,

the colossus, one hand
fumbling stars, the

other whipping comets
at my back. I peer up,

breathless, rub my eyes.
From the shadow of my

smallness cry boldly at
the beauty, at the pain.

The Stranger

He shuffled up, sat down beside
me on the parkbench, removed his
battered hat, remarked on splendors

of a London spring, noting each
flower by name. Pointing to a twisted
pine, saw what I visioned there.

Sensed I was troubled, offered
comfort as he learned my wife was
desperately ill. Uncannily, he

drew from me my past. Then told
me of his life. Shabby philosopher,
he'd traveled everywhere, placed

my accent in midwest America. He
probed on, unraveled things no books
revealed. My son, stirring in his

carriage at my side, made me aware
of time. The stranger rose, hand
on my shoulder. Said I'd be all right,

promised we'd meet again. Years since.
My son now has a small son of his own.
Last summer, in the garden with my

wife, I watched our grandson gathering
cones beneath the pine. Dozed off.
On waking, looked up, saw the stranger

doff his battered hat, seeming well
satisfied. I started, found it
was the breeze making a moving shadow

of a twisted branch. Recalled the
stranger's promise we would meet
again. Come back, a spirit of the pine.

Kanrantei

(Wave Pavilion)

> Spilled from the pines
> of Matsushima,
> crests—charged with cones
> and needles—
>
> fray tasseled ropes circling
> rocks below
> the shrine. Beyond, in
> misted reaches
>
> of the Bay, a flawless scroll.
> Five giant
> guardians of Godaido Temple
> wait on
>
> pilgrims chanting over
> half-moon
> bridges, as waves swell, break
> over Kanrantei.

Willows

(for Taigan Takayama, Zen master)

> I was walking where the willows
> ring the pond, meaning to reflect
> on each, as never before, all
> twenty-seven, examine twig by twig,
> leaf by pointed leaf, those delicate
> tents of greens and browns. I'd
>
> tried before, but always wound up
> at my leafless bole of spine, dead
> ego stick, with its ambitions,
> bothers, indignations. Times
> I'd reach the fifth tree before
> faltering, once the seventeenth.

Then, startled by grinding teeth,
sharp nails in the palm, turn back,
try again. Hoping this time to
focus on each bough, twig, leaf,
cast out all doubts that brought
me to the willows. This time

it would be different, could see
leaves shower from the farthest
tree, crown my head, bless my eyes,
when I awakened to the fact—
mind drifting to the trees ahead.
I was at fault again, stumbling to

the flap of duck, goose, a limping
footstep on the path behind,
sun-flash on the pond. Such excuse,
easy to find, whether by willows
or bristling stations of a life.
Once more, I'm off. This time

all's still. Alone, no one to blame
distractions on but self. Turn in
my tracks, back to the starting point.
Clench, unclench my hands, breathe in,
move off telling the leaves like
rosary-beads, willow to willow. Mind

clear, eye seeing all, and nothing.
By the fifth, leaves open to me,
touch my face. My gaze, in wonderment,
brushes the water. By the seventh,
know I've failed. Weeks now, I've been
practicing on my bushes, over, over again.

Bells of Lombardy (1986)

ONE

Rooms

I.

The casket under the rose
in the funeral parlor is not
where you live, my mother.

Garbling words for father,
sister, son, aunts, brother-
in-law, wife on an alien

stage, I enter a place high
above daffodils, hyacinths,
tulips of neighboring

gardens, where fire-scaled
butterflies wing free among
leaves, as you sit beside me

in tears at the old kitchen
table, dreading the moment I
leave, a young soldier off to

the Pacific in World War II.
I quietly touch your hand, promise
to take care, write often. In

foxholes, opening mail, I see
you daily, sending your life-line
of words from that room. On

my return, I let myself in to
surprise you sorting my letters
like charms on the bright

checkered cloth. This time
tears come with joy. So what
am I doing making my sermon

here? You are outside the window,
looking in, the monarch you
once made a poem, pure spirit,

wings carrying you above the
rose, to calm your children's
and their children's, grief.

II.

Forward observers, fresh
from mission in the hills
of Okinawa, we crawl back

to our foxholes, under
a battle hymn of mortar
flak and fire, charged

with rumor that our president
has died. Ginger, always
skeptic, rubs his three-day

stubble, mutters—
"At least," "On the contrary,"
"Oh yeah!" Hopsi, the clown,

gulps *Aqua Velva* lotion in
despair. Weary, I lie
in my earth-room, just four

feet deep, rest on my
duffle, feeling the outline
of letters from home, Walt

Whitman's *Leaves of Grass*
under my head. I think
of other times, time that

might never be, cry out
for all the dead. As
howitzers split distance,

and the shells aim back, I
stare up wondering at my
roof of shrapnel and stars.

III.

Children's voices strain, round
on round, sweetly breathless,
follow their father, the troubador,

fiddling a chanty in Paris, outside
the church of St. Germain-des-Prés.
The crowd bravos, coins chime on

asphalt. Farther on, a trumpeter
passes his hat in an outdoor café,
where I turn down the street to

the Hôtel de Buci, stop once again
to look into the door. After
thirty-five years, how to explain

to a weary-faced clerk my need
to peer into a room, the size of
a closet, my home for two years

as a GI student back from war.
Trudging there, laden with books,
from the Sorbonne each night, I'd

prop on the sagging bed, back to
one wall, feet up on the other,
stare at the candle's soft flame

in the long dresser mirror. I'd
read through the dictionary, stalking
new words for verse scrawled on

used paper bags, old envelopes
airmailed from home, to the beat
of the asthmatic radiator. How I

would love to climb those stairs once
more, see where it all began. Making
a bold check, in the g's, for granadilla—

where visions of stigmata, nail marks,
thorns became a poem heavy with
may-pops, fruit of the passionflower.

TWO

Bells of Lombardy

I. Bellagio

> On the mountain's side, high among
> wild flowers, finger aimed at the
> typewriter key, I look up, startled:
>
> late May sun through the stained-
> glass window flares the wall with
> mosaics—red, green, yellow, blue.
>
> My room's ablaze over the Chapel
> of the Madonna of Monserrato:
> its faded Virgin and Child above
>
> the tarnished cross, fallen candles,
> stare through the rusted grill. Seems
> only yesterday, back home, cardinals,
>
> bluejays, made a rainbow round the
> feeder, as snowbirds spilled like
> leaves from maples, spruce, calling up
>
> starlings across miles of frozen fields.
> Today I sit where, twenty centuries
> since, Pliny the Younger raised a villa
>
> "proper to the questing mind," rivaling
> ice-speared Alps clear in the distance.
> I imagine the cliff scaled, won, routed
>
> again, squint as a lizard scoots across
> the smudged graffiti by the ledge:
> names, dates, hometowns of former
>
> sojourners—who must have sat here,
> breathless, as the hawks swooped over
> lake-waves shifting in the wind below
>
> the sheer cliff drop. I search for words.

II. Garden

Villa gardeners trudge
from terraces above,
pour basketsful of

cuttings over the cliff-
face, near my door.
Two hundred feet below

the poem withering on
my desk, petals cascade
into a garden on the

waves. Noon: they feast
under the kumquat trees,
bread, olives, cheese

and wine spread on the
checkered cloth. The
gardeners raise their

glasses as I pass. My
morning's crop, beside
their flower-fall, ant

droppings on the page.

III. Dawn

To the east a fishing
boat from Pescallo
drifts north, blue

kettle at the stern
kindled in the early
light. Now it rocks in

time with San Giacomo's
iron birds, clanging the
dawning hour. Boatmen,

back to back with rods
held firm, steady each
other for the catch

they'll share over a
flask on shore. Only
the mountains are older

than this ritual—
over the centuries
they and the sun have

shadowed fishers, and
the fathers of fishers,
seen them come and go.

IV. Madonna

Evening: on the terrace, after
dinner, distracting from sunset
prisming the lake, a stream of light

moves up the mountain path. I
take off for my room, as pilgrims,
candles flickering in colored paper

cones, file down the chapel steps,
begin their song of praise before
the newly polished shrine. A nun,

finger on lips, silences fidgety
children with a smile. The priest
of San Giacomo faces his flock, raises

the golden cross, unfolds the drama
of the loaves and fishes. An old man
leans against the wall, eyes turned

toward the sky, frail voice quivering
the last hymn. As the procession
snuff their candles, start to leave,

a sparkling everywhere—the year's
first fireflies light the last hours
of the Madonna's month. Soon the

chapel will begin to gather dust,
stirred only, now and then, by
the pacing secret sharer overhead.

V. The Terrace

Follow my wife along the narrow
path, beside a wall rainbowed
with flowers rooted in its stone.

Above woods, from the precipice,
we spot plane trees of Cadennabia
across the lake. Cut back through

caverns to the terrace. There join
the others for aperitifs, talk
of our benefactress Ella Walker,

daughter of Hiram, Kentucky's whisky
king. I swap my usual sherry for
a bourbon in honor of the fearless

Gibson girl and Jamesian spirit,
who passing from a Polish prince
and Yankee playboy, became Principessa

della Torre e Tasso. Did she sit
here, below the castle remnants on
the peak, making a charming point

at tea? Or pacing room to room did
memories of Derby Balls, foxhunts across
the bluegrass shadow the Guardis,

Cranach, Cimabue on the walls? Husband
dead, winter ramming the mountain pass,
bust of Pliny the Younger overhead

recast in ice—was it then she chose
to gift this "tower of the mind?"
Raise our glasses, toast her *dolce vita*.

VI. *Plaques*

Descending slope by slope, dazzled
by light off the slate roofs of
Bellagio, I let myself out of the

villa, enter the old road, turning
by Via della Musica to Salita
Serbelloni. On steps moving down

to the lake, souvenir shopkeepers,
bronzed as fine leather, sit by their
wares in the sun. Along the old moat

wall I pause by the tall iron grill of
the Villa Lambertenghi. To the left
of the gate a small plaque recalls

Enrico Genazzini stayed here, making
"a name in the labor movement." To the
right a large plaque shows mercurial

Franz Liszt was here with Madame d'Agoult,
pregnant, it tells, with the future
Cosima Wagner. I step back, imagine

music beyond sound, muffled by bells of
San Giacomo as, here, they circled the
garden, now become "Park of the Martyrs."

Strange how time thrust such spawning
into the hero-bed of Wagner: years
beyond, basking at a tyrant's feet,

Liszt's child inspired those chords
to which jackboots—echoing still—
tramped a generation to its doom.

VII. Motorboats

Dawn rings the mountains
as church bells herald
the fishers' catch to shore.

Out of silence, swift as
wasps stirred in May flowers,
the humming of motorboats.

From Varenna, Mennagio they
split the lake, skimming,
racing, side-swiping sail-

boats, scuttling fish,
paddlers, swimmers. Years,
troubled townspeople raged,

while officials mulled over
ledgers, graphs, weighing the
profit and loss of stern

measures. Cafés rumble,
signatures swell petitions,
papers crackle with letters,

while the bright-painted
streakers buzz through the
water, rivaling the intricate

circling of hawks over slopes
where the Romans raised
villas and, for two millennia,

the waves rang with odes.

VIII. Lizards

Daily, I tread warily the
footpath to my desk. Always
the jeweled periscopes of

heads, soaking up sun, after
night's ice winds off the
Alps. Turning by hedgerows,

a lizard world scrambles,
scoots off, taking me back a
score of years to Khorramshahr,

where with wife and children
in a harem turned hotel, I
watched the lizards on our

earth-floor bedroom wall—
dinosaur shadows in the oil
rig fumes. Over dining tables,

like centurions, they whipped
from dish to dish, defying.
Here, legs spread against rose

trellises, these spirits of the
past flit from the pregnant cat
who stalks their tender young.

IX. Sunday Mass

As the procession moving up
the aisle halts at the last
bell, an old woman in black,

on her knees, turns, stares at me,
whispers, "*Stranieri.*"
Candle to candle, the acolytes

steady their tapers, move back
to the altar. Choir songs
stir the pews, again the old

woman observes me. The priest
raises his head, intones to
the rafters. The old woman

swings round, looks into my
eyes—startled, I see I am
keeping her from her God. The

priest's voice echoes on the
hooped window, where a butterfly
thrusts, flails for salvation.

The priest gestures, deep in
his drama of angels and devils,
while altar girls nudge one

another beside altar boys. Last
hymn set to the rustle and fumble
for coins, I double my pittance

under the old woman's gaze.
Candles snuffed, after the blessing,
we file out into the square,

dazzled by sunlight on cobblestones.
To dodge the old woman, squinting
close by the church wall, I race

by tourists, young folk sipping
coffee in outdoor cafés—
bolt through the traffic, uphill.

X. Lovers

Breezy Sunday afternoon,
surf-riders plow, tail-ending
motorboats criss-crossing

on the lake. In the cove
beneath my window, feet from
the cliff-base, a rowboat

vibrates, sun quivering
through leaves on the man's
back, gilding his buttocks,

dappling the girl's black
hair, leg anchoring his thigh.
An eternity: tremors fade

to stillness, stir again, as
scrambling into swimsuits, they
paddle back to "Rent a Boatride"

on the quay. Drifting to shore
do they go separate ways, under
wrought balconies rambling with

flowers, to dream the cove again—
closer, tightening, rolling on
the wave-surge of another time.

XI. Monday Morning

Early, before the villa and
the town awake with day's
first flush, I greet the

nightwatchman with the gentle
moonlike face, go down the
mountain steps through dawn mist

into shuttered silent streets.
Suddenly, air vibrates with
the tenor aria from *Pagliacci*,

hoarse as Caruso's heartsick
clown. Just beyond, a truck pulls
in, a paunchy driver jumps down,

flings open doors, voice brimming.
He hoists one sack of flour at
a time onto his burlapped shoulder,

unloads them five doors down.
Soon he passes me, full voiced,
along the road to San Giovanni.

Now a girl with a half eaten
roll bursts from an arched footway,
flips crumbs to a striped cat

pawing garbage, turns down to
the bus stop. Within the hour
the first ferry will unmoor,

café terraces will be swabbed,
chairs, tables, menus readied,
trinkets, silk scarves outspread,

tortoiseshell necklaces, enameled
rings, leather keychains, marble
figurines polished—to light

the tourist's eye. As I return,
see the nightwatchman's children
chasing up the slope to meet him.

Wonder if the girl's still waiting
for the bus to Como, whether
the truck driver's song goes on.

XII. In Lombardy

So near Verona: eye centers
beyond peaks silhouetted
in the distance, turns back

centuries to Pisanello, taking
time out from medallions to
paint his *Vision of St. Eustace*,

my thirty year rapture at the
National Gallery, London. Here,
in the clear frame of the sky,

I see Christ crucified across
the antlers of a stag, while
creatures of the earth, this

luminous hour, forage at peace
in rich grass. Today, creators
of bold theories on the mind would

see hallucination where the
artist stroked all suffering in
his saint, who waits, hand raised

before his chest, poised at the
trembling edge, sensing the world's
glinting arrow speeding toward

the stag's, and his own, heart.

XIII. Mist

Bells of San Giovanni
Battista, San Giacomo
strike a roundelay in mist,

lifting here and there
to show what lies between
truth and imagination.

Somnambulist, I watch
scenes come and go: Monte
Tremezzo's tip behind

a void, once Cadennabia.
Varenna, but a fracture in
the ink-washed slopes of

Primo, Crocione and the
fading Alps.
                        As peaks

emerge, drift off, I know
that anything can happen
where all distinctions end.

XIV. Lake Light

Light gilds Lake Como, daubs waves
rippling like ripe corn-stalks
in the fields of Illinois, rainbows

fish surfacing for insects, haloes
the white gulls screaming from
the north. As Monte Tremezzo's

shadow widens, hawks sky-dance,
swoop through burnished olive trees,
where the nightwatchman clears the

bracken on his daytime shift. He
looks up, salutes me with his rake.
Pacing the halls in moonlight, working

the land by day, he envies no one.
"Got a good wife," he says, "fine
children, roof over my head. Work

hard? No need for me to leave family,
cross borders in winter, like most
others, searching in Switzerland,

Belgium to put food on the table."
He sweeps his rake full-circle: "I
watch the seasons come and go, like

light on water. Know I'm a lucky man."

XV. Redwoods

Strolling under redwoods by
the duckpond, tennis court
toward the castle ruins—

from the peak I see Monte
Dongo to the north, recall
that fateful April 1945.

Wonder if spring flowers laced
the hedgerows then, as now,
where—stopped short on its

course—a fleeing limousine
delivered Mussolini, his mistress
Clara and their party to swift

justice, their corpses taken
from Mezzegra, on the road
he'd paved, into Milano. Hung

by his feet in the great public
square, stoned, spat upon by
those trapped in his Grand Design.

They say the cocks of Pescallo
crowed lustily that day, as
thousands—lake to lake—

gathered to mourn their dead.
Life would be good at last,
the *grappa* strongest in memory.

Through those bitter years Californian
redwoods, planted by a princess
from Kentucky, grew some twenty

feet, a fitting roost for hawks.

XVI. Concert

The visiting choir of San Giovanni
di Lecco form an arc behind the pulpit
of San Giacomo. Men's ties, women's

gowns take on the azure of mosaics in
the central apse. The director waits
for a flustered latecomer to settle,

nods, lifts arms. His baton weaves
clear voices, rapt in 16th century
sacred song, in and out the columns

of black Varenna marble, up to the
dome. The pure tones of the young
soprano, score hugged to her breast,

radiant as the Miraculous Madonna on
the wall of the right aisle, waver
on a high note. Altar lilies, jeweled

gladioli catch medieval echoes of tenors,
counter-tenors, mezzos, basses, haloing
the air—forty miles from La Scala.

After the last note, the applause, the
young soprano, gown luminous in soft light,
runs to embrace her mother. The chorus

files out. Silent, we exit into the wind,
lightning spearing the lake, thunder
sounding through the whole of Lombardy.

XVII. Swallows

No rain for twenty days,
and summer yet to come.
Under jade foliage we watch

the ferries ease to shore:
cameras round their necks,
the tourists in short-shorts

snap each other, sipping
caffè latte, licking *gelati*,
spooning strawberries and

cream beside the lake. Up
here, sprinklers on, even
villa gardeners hug shade,

muttering *caldo*, as cool
wings of swallows dip and
point. They arrow, loop

rings around each other,
down-tailing for gnats—
sheer joy in mountain light.

Air thick with roses, buzzed
by stippled hornets nesting
on the wall, we gather over

sherry greened by cypresses.

XVIII. *Park of the Martyrs of Liberty*

Downhill, I pass snails opaling the way,
saunter by waterfalls of miniature
snapdragon. Entering the square of

San Giacomo, I am confronted by a name
on the old convent wall: Teresio Olivelli,
patriot, tortured, murdered in Hersbruk Camp,

aged 29. Restless, I question friends,
officials, strangers—who shrug, as if
so much reality could only blight a poem.

I stalk for traces, ferret out of silence
a poet-professor, officer of the famed
Alpine unit routed on the Russian front,

who, given up for lost, outflanked a blizzard,
two wounded comrades in his arms: bemedaled
National hero, recovering by this shore,

illusions fizzled in clear light on water.
He joined, reorganized the freedom-
fighters. Betrayed, imprisoned, twice escaped,

betrayed again, comforting fellow inmates
to the last. His "Prayer of the Rebel" lived
on. "We were rebels for love," he said.

Going back up through the public garden,
I pause where German tourists picnic,
lean against a rock bearing three names:

Teresio Olivelli, partisan, killed by Nazis,
17.1.45;
Tino Gandola, partisan, shot down in the street,
aged 18, 9.7.44;
Ninetto Gilardoni, partisan, slain in savage
combat at Vallsolda, 29.11.44.

The tourists' children climb the rock,
bombard their fathers with blood-red azalea
petals, as guidebooks in hand, day-trippers

shadow footprints of Liszt and his lady,
unaware this garden is a shrine to greater
love. I rest upon a bench nearby, recalling

Saipan, Okinawa, fallen friends. More
than an hour I sit here—
watching the blind go by, in martyrs' park.

XIX. Poppies

This morning villa paths
explode into a Flanders-scape
of poppies. Crinkly orange

soft, they open with the day.
I pluck one, turn its bristly
stem, kaleidoscope four silken

petals, sniff the musky odors
of another time and place.
A Persian corner, near the

Imam Reza's Shrine, where opium
from white and scarlet flowers
was bartered in the long blue

shadow of the minaret. Retaste
a single pipeful, readied
by a friend, which left me

headachy and wiser. I twirl
the poppy back into this moment,
raise it to the light. Petals

fly off, leaving pistil rays,
all set to cast a shower of
seed into the first lake breeze.

XX. *Choice*

Clear air greens slopes across
the lake, shimmers at the point
dividing wind. Gold/blue linens,

lacquered wardrobe, blues, reds,
greens and ochres of the Persian
prayer rug on our bedroom wall

are burnished by the first rays
of the sun. Later, the dining
room's a-buzz with conference guests

exploring socio-psychological
effects of chaos over breakfast
rolls and juice. I sit beside

an expert on Disasterology, spoon
bran flakes as he sums up catastrophic
floods, wars, earthquakes—

desperately cut my omelette, stare
into a crater, gulp the remnants
of a sliding world. Outside,

breathe deep the quiet scent of
flowers, tramp past my study to
the precipice. Recall sad friends,

each with his own disaster, leaping
from some edge. And the old gardener
our host Roberto spoke of, aiming

his basket of rose-cuttings from
the spot I stand on now, who lost
his balance, and some three days

later was sighted face down in the
water. How stormy was his life
that morning, a split second from

the end? Nowhere else to go, was
he overcome by red, yellow, pure white
petals floating on green waves?

XXI. Crumbs

Along one of the villa's hundred
paths, I reach the spot where
bamboo dips into the half-moon pond.

Under the relics of the castle walls,
shaded by redwoods, sycamores, I
toss lunch-crumbs to pucker-mouthed

goldfish, flash-orange fins translucent
as the spiderweb traced on the
bamboo fringe brushing the water,

where two mallards glide out from
the grotto, move as one, as one
feed lazily. Tempted to stir their

sweet monogamy, hurl my offerings
far, this way and that. Calmly they
steer from one side to the other.

Feast done, satisfied, they turn tail,
drift back to their secret place.
I forge on uphill, from the lofty

point view the maze of paths carved
out by men Duke Alessandro salvaged
in the 1815 famine. Like bees

they tunneled through the cliff,
cut winding shelves from stone,
grateful for a Duke who cared enough

to swap his fortune for a starving
horde—a daily bowl of cornmeal
mush, crumbs between life and death.

XXII. *Morning Rain*

Deep in my Roman bathtub
I lie back, listening to
rain pelting the veranda,

watch dawn misting trees
above the orange villa on
the slope across the way.

I hold the moment close,
outline the scene. Downstairs
a glumness rises from the

table, edges the reading
nook. Windows, doors are
closed, lamps lighted in

the gloom. Murmurs of
canceled boat trips, tennis
matches fill the corridor.

Help myself to an umbrella.
On my way bright lizards
scurry by, hawks swoop

for creatures lured out
by the flood. Back
at my desk, face to face

with myself, try to set down
words, as morning shifts
like haze upon the lake.

XXIII. Gardener

Outside the door the gardener
greets me, as always,
with the latest weather news,

laughing as I take off, bowed
in concentration—
"Scrive, sempre scrive!"

Somehow I know he wants me
to do well, to honor the
Madonna's Chapel where, since

sunrise, I've been trying to
type a season fresh as his.
Daily I watch him planting,

weeding, pruning, caring for
young transplanted lemon
trees. I dodge the sprinklers

circling my footsteps as I
pass his seedlings on the
greenhouse ledge. Imagine

how I'll miss him back where
no one but my wife heeds what
I do. Will he miss the stranger

searching for a splendor
along borders, with little
hope of wonders such as his?

XXIV. Fireworks

Closing my book, sit with my wife
on the veranda, enjoy the quiet of
sundown. Children's voices rise

amidst the town's slate roofs. A
stray bird wings through twilight
beyond silhouettes of olive, kumquat,

cypress trees. Faint music and the
sound of revelers draw near—
a pleasure yacht, decked out with

pennants, harbors in close view.
Our solitude's perked up with
dancing, laughter, clinking glasses,

find our feet tapping as the dark
sets in. Slowly they move toward
the center of the lake, anchoring

there. A stillness, then a rush of
fireworks bursts up from the shore,
a rainbow showers. Soon streamered

lights reflect a ghost-ship until,
suddenly, a tenor starts out—
Za za, za za! An instant, I'm a child

back on the south side of Chicago,
envying my buddy Jiggs Venturini for
the wine and pasta odors from his

kitchen door, and for his grandfather,
who spoke no English, cranking the
handle of the gramophone to play old

Neopolitan folk songs out on the porch
those lazy summer nights. Now, as
then, I join in heartily, *Za za, za za!*

XXV. Bamboo

At this point on the mountain,
feeling the ridges of a cool-
grey bamboo stalk, I might be

rambling down beyond the lake,
along the road to Loppia,
passing raked sand, fine stone

lanterns, stunted pines and
the same reedy clumps behind
the railings of the Villa Melzi.

Or a continent away, west on
Honshu Island, I might be parting
hollow stems to reach a hut

abandoned by some hermit near
the Joei Temple. Standing
in the shadow of the Kirin Range,

listening to a distant water-
wheel turning my life, place by
place, moment by moment, up to

this hour when I touch the woody
grass, in wonder of its hungry
roots thrusting through forests,

valleys, gardens to this mountain.

XXVI. Lilies: Last Day

Yesterday wind blasted gulls
gliding for pickings on the
surging foam. Today air's

soft and warm, lake water
smooth as petals opening
everywhere. White, bronze,

tiger-orange lilies frame
the passage where, for the
last time, I reach my study

door. Take in, once more,
hawks ranging over the
Madonna's Chapel, the blazing

window-wheel, the shelves
of land above, the drop
below. Begin to understand

why Pliny called his villa
Tragedia: perched on
this edge the actors come and

go, while creatures swoop
and dart, the flowers bloom
and die, and come again.

Tomorrow we'll be dropped at
Como Station, take the train
part way to our own place.

Long after, sitting at my
old oak desk, before the
window, I'll look out beyond

the spruce and maples, trace
a lizard sunning on a mountain
path, a burgeoning of lilies.

Of Pen and Ink and Paper Scraps (1989)

ONE: FROM THE WINDOW

Luck—1932

After the market crash, everyone
short on luck, I squinted out
my bedroom window for the last time,

holding the rabbit's foot I'd
swopped my slingshot for, counted
numbers for a miracle that wouldn't

come. As the last mock-orange
petal in Andrade's yard spun into
summer, the junkman divvied up

our table, chairs, beds, all we
could not cart off from Chicago, for
a piddling sum. Clutching my can

of marbles, baseball mitt, I followed
mother lugging my baby sister,
worldly goods stuffed in a canvas

bag. Tracking my father, job to
job, St. Louis to Columbus. All
that year I made spells, counting

heads, trees, fireflies, polished my
wishbone seven times, again. Until
I landed back in the old city,

raced to Washington Park, joined my
playmates, Shorty, Tonsils, Mike,
riding Taft's human pyramid of *Time*.

As I explained how luck had brought
us back, I found real magic, twigs
sparkling into flower before my eyes.

Black Monday

(NYC, October 1987)

After an early morning trek
under a spill of trees
anchored in rock, where sky-
beams blue as chicory outline

palisades along the Hudson's
bank across the way, I take
the A-train down to 42nd Street.
Across the aisle a young man

beats a rhythm with his feet,
mouthing the rap. As we speed
on, faster, even faster goes
his song. Indifferent to eyes

blinking over headlines of the
market crash, faces grim
as bogs, his soul's raw poem
belts out its need from stop

to stop. Doors open, slam and
open. He takes off, jiving
down the platform toward
gray streets of unending sound.

Light

There comes a moment, turning
a corner sharply, I run
into a young delivery boy on

his first summer job, carting
kegs of white lead, cans of paint
in a red wagon, once his toy,

to patrons of his father's store.
Passing the quips and clowning
of his one-time friends, munching

his wage of cookies, apples, candy,
pocketing a nickel at some doorway
now and then. There comes a time

I see my own face in that twelve
year old, steering his cargo by
the blind man with a caged canary

pecking fortunes typed on colored
paper for a dime. Tempted to stop
he scoots along, afraid to know

how places will dissolve in
time, turn up fifty years later in
a certain light, here on my desk.

My Father Reading

Whenever I catch my father
nodding over endless books—

Grass, Montherlant, Moravia,
Camus—I wonder what he read

the day my mother, who had seen
the stern-eyed soldier at

his desk while on some long-
forgotten errand for a brother,

turned up at the army camp to
entertain the conscripts with

her joyous recitation of folk
poems. Was it that night her

image leapt from some page of
philosophy or art—

led to the moment I could voice
their lives in this brief somg.

From the Window

After night's news stories:
senseless slaughter,
politicking, hunger, waste,

with hype and sport thrown
in, once more to wake
as sun kindles the linden,

lilac, willow-oak, catches
the red-cap drilling layered
membrane of the old pear bark.

So many seasons' rounds of
twig, bud, flower, fruit
have made a banquet for this

stiff-tailed guzzler, now
well slaked, strut-drumming
on a branch to lure his mate.

Dreaming to Music

Windstorm thrums
the window, drizzles
the maple's flame.

So begins another
summer's end. As I
turn up the stereo

a girl in Rheims
walks out of a medieval
love song, lifts

her brocaded gown
along the mucky path
out of the woods,

shortcutting through
a wheatfield silvered
in cloudburst, toward

the farmhouse gate.
Flicking the latch she
looks back, whispers

her passion to the rain,
this Sunday afternoon,
six centuries late.

Scrap Paper

I'm strapped into the oral
surgeon's bogey-chair. The scene
of Northern woods upon the wall

swirls into years of pipe smoke
as the needle hits the dark
vein of my hand, sends me groping

over mounds of textbook
galley sheets, generously donated
by a friend. The brambled

type threads business jargon
through my images, whips pines,
percentiles, graphs into one puff.

So much for more than thirty years
of fine-cut Latakia, sweet
Virginia. As finger-printed carbons

fill my lesioned roof of mouth,
I choke off dark, somehow to
find a clearing where I stumble on

the arms of wife and son, back to
a woozy world of masks made up
of pen and ink and paper scraps.

New Roof

Tarred roof's done: now squirrels,
birds can stop off as they please.

Rap of crabapple, twig, descant
of sleet and gale won't frazzle us again.

Sipping tea, I contemplate old rain-
spots on the ceiling, tune smugly

into newscasts brewing storms. My
peace is startled by wild sounds

behind the furnace-closet door. Wonder
what poor ghost would bother with

a house lacking a basement or dark
winding stairs. Open up, warily look

around, follow a trail of feathers to
a songless wren cowed in the chimney

corner. I open windows, doors, pull
off the screens. Coax, plead and point

the way. Offer my palm. I stalk it,
scoop it tenderly, set it outside before

the maple. Watch it soar, then flounder
back to earth, where from the bushes

a marauding tabby pounces. Later,
I find a tawny feather in the grass.

Misty Morning

The bluejay leaps in/out
vague rakings of the long ago.

Brief photos skelter by,
so many squirrel generations

back in time. Our children
once again are those small

armfuls we might dream would
stay. Our son, racing me

up the mountain path (I let
him sprint ahead), to reach

the Shinto Shrine. Joyfully
there he tries to capture

bubbles of reflected light
between his hands. The memory

turns. I'm sledding with our
girl, warmed by her spirit.

Down she tumbles, laughing,
auburn hair like flame against

the snow. Deep in this sacred
album mists rise, fall about

the trees that are, that were—
cover the distance of our

paths, now that the years
have made us what we are.

Star

Easing out of the garage
toward the emptied garbage
cans field-basing barbered
lawns, ceramic doodads, shrubs,
petunias and geranium beds

half circling downhill, I pull
up sharply as the red-haired
girl across the street turns
up the volume of her boom-box
to full blast, limps out into

the pathway, flexing the braces
on her gammy knees, spits
in her mitt, eager to be
first woman in the baseball
Hall of Fame. Touched by

her gesture, as if she's asking
why the world won't stop to
play, I pull up to the curb,
shut off the motor and, despite
the fussbudget behind the louvered

blinds next door, I nab a fast
one, watch the bittersweet
surprise turn to anticipation,
taking on her pop-idol's
applause as she dreams, base

to base, her first homerun.

Wind Chime

Wind stirs a bonfire of
October maples. I take off
with my daughter, son, his

wife and son, for woods on
Indian river. Years we've
trespassed through this maze

of creatures, sharing wild
grapes, walnuts, mushroom
puffs. Tangling with hail-fellow

mosquitoes. Tracked through
snowdrifts, storms, up to this
stand of poplars, listening

to wind-chime icicles. Today
as autumn shreds and patches up,
we hear the strumming leaves,

watch branches weaving light
into the clouds, know each time
we return might be the last.

Walkers

In sun, in snow, after dawn's
daily dozen on the page,
I shove off down the hill,

take in the same three walkers
circling the park, alongside
gopher lookouts in the scrub.

Safe from the news, day's
tally of brutality and greed,
I catch an acorn's fall, step

over a leaf, nod at the old
man with the fat, lame dog
in tow, smile at the woman

in the sweatsuit with the sad
drawn face, wave as the middle-
ager, bobbing to his headphones,

passes by. Along the quiet
path thoughts fracture, fly
to where a flock of crows mob

a lone owl reflecting in the oak.

Garage Sale

. . . so the nightmare enters
where I wait the rummagers

hunched in a beat-up lawnchair,
feet astride the oil-smudge

on the floor. A car pulls up,
a critic's eyes lynx through

the windshield and the motor
churns, roars off. Well,

I'm just a jingler sharing
the dust with spiders, come

with over sixty years of
misplaced images, not everybody's

bargain. A whitehaired couple
drop in, regard me with suspicion—

what a pity I am not their long
lost son. Take me, I say. Come

buy nothing for nothing, poems
thrown in free. As they fade out

I take the garage sale sign
down, hope for a better day.

Latest News

The Hubbard Glacier, 80 miles
long, 360 feet tall,
is splitting from Alaska,

threatening ocean levels,
sending tremors through
the markets of the world.

Seas will flush out factories,
centuries of masterworks,
blueprints for doom into

the sludge. Igloo and mansion,
barrack and doss-house will
make a new Atlantis, moldy

with warheads, yo-yos, monuments
stockpiling barnacles,
leaving no trace. Sanctuaries

are tipped off to go under,
sending waves of walrus, polar
bear and sprat over seawalls.

Meanwhile as the glacier surges
14 yards a day, ticker-tapes
snake onto desks of speculators,

land values of mountains swell
their dreams. From the Rockies,
Alps, the Urals up to Katmandu,

who knows—if cities, forests,
valleys disappear—Mount Ararat
might come into its own again.

May Day

With spring flowers,
year by year, I watch
the pretty youngster from

the house behind our yard
tiptoeing past the window,
leaving a May-basket at

our door. This time a
paper cone with golden
streamers, colored candies,

chocolate kisses, gum
and purple lilac, to delight
us for the day. Such quiet,

such innocence. Yet each
year brings her closer
to the instant when despair

butts in on joy, opens
the window on harsh May
Days, where empty baskets

hold the hunger of a world.

Theo

Old folk squinting on a bench
    outside the Lodge,
hands folded, feet in line,

shrink into afternoon, like
    Michelangelo's
snowmen carved for a famous

garden on a vain Medici's whim.
    They perk up
as my grandson greets them,

whizzing by on his red bike—
    fleeting reminder
of a small boy round the corner

of their years. Soon he'll grow
    off from us,
this eight year old, his violin

bow already drifting from a squeaky
    exercise into
Bach minuets. I'll miss our

secret tales—audacious clowns,
    mischievous bears.
Quick-freeze his laughter, goodnight

kisses for the day I lean,
    ice-sculptured
on some bench, waiting the thaw.

Daffodils, Irises

My wife's gift—

a birthday halo,
yellow/purple,
trembling from
the Yamaguchi vase
upon my desk.

Saying, year by
year find words
to equal these,
beyond the fallen
petal, withered stalk.

Thoughts before Travel

Baggage stacked and labeled,
phone, cable-television cut off,
disconnecting our small lodging

from the world, I wait the ride
into the airport in the backyard
by the trees. Snip-snipping

of a neighbor's shears, first
spring cough of a mower grow
remote, as bluebird, redbird

sky-dance over iris, and a rabbit
bolts under the grapevine tangle
by the garden shed. Moments of

past journeys stir with laughter
of our children as we pitch on narrow
benches in a third-class carriage

from Bombay up to the Elephanta Caves.
Or enter gardens of raked sand
and stone, stroll under pines to

picnic in the shade of the great
Kamakura Buddha. Follow a desert,
tracing Assassin castles into Zahidan.

Rambling on, a car horn blasts me
back into our rhubarb jungle where
frogs, gorging insects, croak farewell.

June 5, 1987

While I wash dishes to
Gregorian chants, what
started out a ho-hum
day—the usual round

of doodles, chores,
anxieties—explodes
with a bright swallowtail
joyriding by the window,

looping where by whitest
columbines a robin, head
cocked to love sounds,
watches as a squirrel

near the old pear tree
quivers astride his mate.

The phone rings, bringing
word Shinkichi Takahashi

died last night.
                    And so
the world goes on. Now
the squirrels scamper

through the branches,
making leaves dance
like the poet's sparrows
wing-stroking an elegy in air.

Translating Zen Poems

(I. M. Takashi Ikemoto)

The sliding doors open in
the house hugging the mountain-
side where my children sled

in sandpapered orange-crates,
downswoop into our garden under
snow-glazed cypress, walnut,

fig, persimmon trees, mowing
dried stalks of tall eulalia
grass along the way. Inside,

we sit crosslegged, flushed
with hibachi embers, before
the plum-black Sado vase,

under your gift, the Taiga
scroll plum-blossoming out of
season. Over green tea and sweet

bean cake, I watch you shuffling
pages where I've englished
sparrows, temple gardens, fish,

time, universe—waiting
your word.
                Now, thumbing through

years of those poems, I see you,
old friend, in flickering
light of sunset over snow-roofs

of this midwest town, recall
a moment under a mountain, when we
knew a master's words need never die.

TWO

ISSA: A SUITE OF HAIKU

Passing wild geese,
lighting night
mountains of Shinano.

Even in warmest
glow, how
cold my shadow.

Welcome,
wild geese—
now you are Japan's.

In spring rain
how they carry on,
uneaten ducks.

Over fading
eulalia,
cold's white ghost.

Snowy fields—
now rice is down,
more geese than men.

Vines tight
around scorched rocks—
midday glories.

Moist spring moon—
raise a finger
and it drips.

Cooling melon—
at a hint of footsteps,
you're a frog.

My village
traced through haze—
still an eyesore.

Good world—
grass field swollen
with dumplings.

Silverfish escaping—
mothers,
fathers, children.

Sprawled like an X—
how carefree,
how lonely.

Melting snow—
the village flows
with children.

Winter's here—
around the fire,
stench of gossip.

Telescope—
eyeful of haze,
three pence.

Dawn—fog
of Mt. Asama spreads
on my table.

"Gray starling!"
they sneer behind me,
freezing the bone.

House burnt down—
fleas
dance in embers.

My old home—
wherever I touch,
thorns.

Rustling
the grassy field—
departing spring.

Fuji dusk—
back to back,
frogs are chanting.

Far over the
withered field,
light from a hut.

My limbs sharp
as iron nails,
in autumn wind.

Watch out,
young sparrows—
Prince Horse trots close.

Each time I swat
a fly, I squint
at the mountain.

Back gate opens
itself—
how long the day.

Evening—above
kitchen smoke and my
poor knees, wild geese!

Playing stone,
frog lets
the horse sniff.

Don't kill the fly—
it wrings
its hands, its feet.

High on the hill,
I cough
into the autumn gust.

Great moon
woven in plum scent,
all mine.

Song of skylark—
night falls
from my face.

After night in
the dog's bowl,
butterfly scoots off.

Cherry blossoms
everywhere: this
undeserving world.

Frog and I,
eyeball
to eyeball.

Winter moon—
outer moat
cracks with cold.

Woodpecker on
the temple pillar—
die! die! die!

What a moon—
if only she were here,
my bitter wife.

My thinning hair,
eulalia grass,
rustling together.

Plum in bloom—
the Gates of Hell
stay shut.

Charcoal fire—
spark by spark,
we fade too.

Morning glory—
whose face
is without fault?

Wonderful—
under cherry blossoms,
this gift of life.

New Year's Day—
blizzard of
plum blossoms.

Snail—baring
shoulders
to the moon.

My empty face,
betrayed
by lightning.

Into the house
before me,
fly on my hat.

Snail—
always
at home.

Temple gong frozen—
this side of the mountain
I shiver in bed.

Snail, finding
the path
to my foot.

Where in the galaxy
does it wait,
my wandering star?

Autumn wind—
once, it too
was fresh.

Splash—
crow into
white dew.

Sadness of cool
melons—two days
nobody's come.

Autumn mountain—
"We're still alive up here,"
boom temple gongs.

Evening cherry blooms—
is today
really yesterday?

Strong wind—
dog drags
two samurai.

Moonlit wall—
frozen shadow
of the pine.

Bright moon,
welcome to my hut—
such as it is.

Milky Way—windbags
in the capital
struck dumb by you.

Shower: caught in
lightning flash—
me, the death-hater.

Poor winter village—
frosted on notice-board:
"No charity."

Summer field—
thunder,
or my empty stomach?

Cool breeze,
tangled
in a grass-blade.

Short night: snoring
under trees, on rocks—
traveling priests.

Plum blossom branch—
moon urges me
to steal you.

Plum scent—
guests won't mind
the chipped cup.

Praying mantis—
one hand
on temple bell.

Haze swirling
the gate—
who comes?

Light haze—
his sedge hat
waving goodbye.

World of dew?
Perhaps,
and yet. . . .

THREE
THE BLUE TOWER

Three Saints of Nardo di Cione

(painted in Florence, 1350)

What an eye for color! I remember
those three saints in softest
green, rose, blue flushed robes

staring raptly at me—as if
we were close-knit, elbows touching,
silent together 650 years. Have

they mused on this selfsame face
over the ages, through tyrannies,
uprisings, famines, searching in

the wrong place for the Fountain
of Forever? Unlike these park-
squatter pigeons, whirring content

past the lily-pond by late-summer
goatsbeard, from bench to bench,
cocksure of offerings. Soon they

will take off, soar beyond nests
in thick trees to the shoulders
of saints, feathers soft green,

rose and blue, in unfading light.

Salvator Rosa (1615–73)

Strong sun on the Tuscan
town where he painted
did not flush the somber

face of his revolutionist
(that head meant for axing)
propped on the easel, rough

hands unrolling a banner
with—goosequilled in
haste—"Silence, unless

what you have to say
is better than silence."
As sunlight entangled the

hills inquisitors ranted,
rebellion was whispered in
shade. Rosa worked on, deepening

eyes of his saints, risking
slogans on canvas. And
that was better than silence.

Modern Art

The lumpish woman
with such grief carved
in her face, cardigan

stretched out of shape
draping her rounded
shoulders over a bargain-

basement dress, stands
in a corner of the
gallery, indifferent

to know-alls solving
nothing before Pollocks,
Klines, De Koonings,

stopping by to touch
her, snigger at her need
to find the Way Out

of this bitter world,
crumble back to
powder, start again.

Fame

Snow on chalet roofs dazzles
as the Paris-Rome Express
scorches the passes. Crammed

with a Turkish widow and her
pouting son in a couchette,
I sip her offering, a paper

cup of wine, answer questions
vaguely, staring out at Swiss Alps
candling the sky. "To Florence,

and alone, for Dante? Ha!"
Suddenly she points a finger
at me, says, "My friend, there

is a Turkish poet greater . . .
taller than these mountains
over pigmy rocks." Stirred

by her passion the boy forgets
to whine, fidgets with glee.
She hands me pen and paper—

"Your address," she says, "I'll
send . . . you'll see!" I
drain the cup, decline another

drop. Lean back and close my
eyes until we reach the border.
Watch her take off, boy in tow.

She turns back, waves, and calls—
"You'll see. There's no one like
him. Never . . . never will be."

Venice

Boozy on art, I savor
my *espresso* at an outdoor
cafe in St. Mark's Square.

Observe the camera touts
snapping peanut vendors
as they hustle tourists among

pigeons, under the unflinching
eye of a winged lion
and St. Theodore astride

his crocodile. As six
musicians strike a barcarole
I squint at light on

stone, the roundabout
of faces as sun slips
down cathedral columns.

Dozing off, I am Francesco
Guardi painting out
the four bronze horses

from the tiered roof of
St. Mark's, down to the
square, where I must return

them over the canals
to Constantinople—
there my canvas waits.

The Savior of Hyde Park

Years, at Speaker's Corner,
he offered reason to
the crowds, at a respectful

distance on a crate he'd
bought for sixpence from
a tout. Shuffling ideas

on weather, politics, art,
war, old Shakespeare
and the like, he held sway

over "Hear hears," "Quite
Sos," hecklers. An encore for
a handshake was his rule.

Squinting at notes to check
a point, thumbs in lapels,
he'd pause for laughs or cheers.

Until the mood changed with
the times—sneers, insults,
lewd remarks forced his escape.

Nowadays he stands alone upon
his perch, tattered notes rolled
tightly in one hand, the other

at his chest. Silent, he
stares out at an audience of
trees, a sculpture of a man

returned to save the world.

Legacy

I look outside where the once
scurvy crook-shaped plot,
cooped by a stark brick wall—

breathing space of semi-basement
flats—has turned into
an Eden. Think of the grayhaired

woman up in Number 8, who
three years earlier shrugged at
apartment-ruled "off limits,"

neighbors' slights behind
drawn curtains. Set to
with spade and trowel, digging,

planting, watering seedlings,
pointing out sproutings to her
old lamed husband, stooping to

weed, pick up a cigarette butt
contemptuously aimed. Widowed
since, gone to a "sheltered lodge,"

I wonder if she's thinking this
midsummer of a wall ablaze with
roses, lupines, daisies, pinks,

hydrangeas shimmering like
stained glass against worn brick?
Now from behind those windows,

drapes flung wide, the undeserving
gape, where fragrant and bee-
swarmed, buds open to the sun.

Friends

Arm in arm the two men
enter Regent's Park,
cross the bridge of flared

geraniums, horned lupines
and the trail of lavender
to the stone-shelved

waterfall, pausing to
chat under a thatch of
willow. Then on to lush

Bird Island, gesturing
where duck families
pass fiery-beaked black

swans close by the reeds.
The blind man glances
through his friend's eyes

at the sweetpea trellis,
flush of roses, madcap
columbines. Settling on

a bench they shower crumbs
to birds, rejoice together
as a sparrow chances on the

blind one's outstretched hand.

Hove Beach

(after John Constable)

> The woman in the wide-
> brimmed hat down on
>
> the beach, squints over
> the surf, no longer in
>
> hope of reunion. Her
> boy, in starched sailor
>
> suit, still believes
> the world he maps out
>
> in the sand will survive
> the walloping tides.
>
> As sunset dissolves
> in waves, the painter
>
> dips his brush in
> the wash of horizon,
>
> sends fishing boats
> over the canvas edge.

Bacchus

> Coaxing a skirl from
> his harmonica, the tippler
>
> in the grime-stiff coat
> riling commuters by
>
> the station gate, two-steps
> backwards off the curb,

rights himself, shakes
windmill fists at life,

the world, the mob who
will not pause to throw

a pittance, to tot up
his night. Blowed if he

cares just how they waste
their lives, shoving in

and out of doors rigged up
to slam shut in one's

face. It serves them
right, snubbing a thirsty man.

Landscape

Over the twilight field
the lost, the fortunate
have wandered paths,
slowly exited the gates,

yet flute-notes hover in
the outlined plane trees,
latticed reflections
of the sky, crisscrossed

by gulls that drift close
to the young man sprawled
on a park bench, flute
bronzed in sun's last rays.

From zoo cages, just over
the fence, roarers,
bleaters, trumpeters answer,
each with his simple need.

Surprise

While his mother sunbathes
full-length on the grass
beside the lily-pond in

St. John's Garden, the small
boy begs rose cuttings of
the gardener snipping among

August beds. His hands flutter
over the basket like twin
butterflies as he picks out

red, orange, yellow petals,
sniffing each windfall in
delight. Hands full, he frisks

back to his mother, places
them gently on her legs, arms,
makes a garland for her hair.

Night Music

The artist rousing a Chopin
polonaise on stage, at Royal
Festival Hall, is tuned out
of the drama stirring under

the concrete columns below,
the hum of the anywhere-sleepers
bearing their worldly
bundles, their cardboard cots.

Settling in chosen corners
out of the wind, these minstrels
of hazy wine-moons nod off
as a fiddler close by the bridge

waits on the concert crowd's
exit, the generous few, tunes up
his strings, sets his cap down
and fingers a waltz to the river.

Drama

The white hairpiece he
wears for his part
in the play down the road

is no disguise for the
veteran actor slipping
unnoticed into a rear seat

at a rival's matinee.
Collar up, he improvises
a fresh plot where, as

lights dim, a swarm of
eager faces turn back from
the stage to cheer him

through his consummate role—
funny, relentless, spell-
binding, drawing their

laughter, sighs, bravos with
a mere gesture. As the curtain
rises and the scene takes

shape, he knows the audience
he loved for loving him
have found a new face to betray.

Images

I

Glimpsed through
rushes fringing

the duckpond isle,
a Japanese

lantern feathered
with goosedown,

image capsized
in water-light.

Ruffling before it
a young gray-lag

gander beats
territorial waves.

II

The train jolts me
to an awareness

of gulls, hundreds
of them, fresh from

oil-rig furrows of
the North Sea. They

dive to barley fields,
close to the plow

churning black waves
from earth—

then veer to clouds
with their spoil.

Botanist

(Sweden, 1986)

The season leaning into
winter in Uppsala, my friend
Lennart and I

warm up with coffee in
a second-floor cafe. Look
out the window

at the year-end remnants
of Linnaeus' Garden, speak
of the harmony

of rows, the rage for order.
Remembering the Latin cry
for Clarity, I

see now what I lack, wonder
why this handsome young
translator of plays

and poems chose to take on
a voice lost in wild and
unnamed grasses where

birds, so namelessly alive,
return from unknown regions every
spring, to swoop

where gold untitled flowers
light leaf-fossils through
old winter's mud.

Fishing with Casper

(Sweden, 1986)

Ringed by shadow-heads of pines
we drift over Stromaren, Lake of Storms,
in bright nippy air, trailing

Old Pike, the one who never fails
to get away. Casper gives
the rod to me, hoping for stranger's

luck, rows us from point to point
where, he says, fish abound. As
the line grows heavy I pull in my catch,

a clump of tangled reeds. Through
the swift-darkening afternoon, forest
closing in, my friend consoles me,

certain there will be no fish-fry
back in Orbyhus tonight, where his wife
and children wait us in their sprawling

house inside the castle grounds. There,
over schnapps, sharp herring, moose,
crisp tart snowberries we laugh together,

chat of icefishing and poems, canny pike
and bass, still warmed by light-arrows
piercing water, a moment of October sun.

The Blue Tower

(Sweden, 1986)

Uninvited, up in the Blue Tower
we touch four years of a man's
life. Strindberg's last home,
on Drottninggatan: those

stage-prop rooms, rigidly ordered
desk, photos of wives, a laurel
wreath framing his youngest child,
cheap casts of artists that he

must have loved one time, third-
rate wallhangings—caves, fluted
columns, backdrops for scenes—,
shadows of masterworks. And all

the rivalries, a melancholia
that poisoned fame, seeping through
doors, following into afternoon
streets of Old Stockholm. On

to evening at the Royal Theater
where I feel Miss Julie's passion,
in a language I can't follow, more
intense than ever. Watch the spit-

booting servant edge from cunning
into scorn, catch the rancor in him,
the despair in her. Outside, walking
with friends back to my lodging,

we pass where Olof Palme, strolling
out of a theater with his wife, met
his assassin. On that very spot
his mourners place fresh roses every day.

Before a Reading

(On the Day of the Mini-Summit, October 11, 1986)

To turn away, not to be overcome
here in Sweden, quietest of lands,

as earth opens in San Salvador
swallowing rightists, leftists,

whipping the rage of 60,000 perished
in civil war into one scream—

will they turn away? Or pause
to remember the quake last year

in Mexico City, leaving an old man
blinking through space, once home,

weeping for songs left unsung by
children, grandchildren? Will they

black out the volcano spilt over
orchards bursting with sweetness

for 400 years in Colombia, where all
that remained was the petrified

arm of a woman reaching from lava
in hope? Is it to warn, this ice-rain

mantling shoulders of those gone
to barter the world in Reykjavik

while wolves prowl pine mountains
of Nerrbotten, howl at an empty sky?

From *Cage of Fireflies:*
Modern Japanese Haiku (1993)

Crow perched
in winter grove—
How far I've come!

Fura (1888–1954)

First thing to catch my ear—
stream
of my native village.

Hosha (1885–1954)

Autumn wind—in my heart,
how many mountains,
how many rivers.

Insects, village lights,
longing
for each other.

Slighted
by the falcon's eye—
man in the field.

Garden stones,
all day long,
forever.

Exiting the Great Gate
of the harsh Zen temple,
flower of arrowroot.

Aging—
more haiku,
more turnip broth.

Kyoshi (1874–1959)

Late cicadas—
how much longing
in their song.

Red dragonfly
seeking company,
lands on my shoulder.

Full autumn moon—
I too am quite well,
as you see.

Soseki (1867–1916)

Daily, flesh
gets thinner,
bones more thick.

How calming
after rage—
shelling of peas.

Loneliness—
my nails grow
longer, longer.

Hosai (1885–1926)

Night—over
sleeping children,
sound of the waves.

Hakusen (20th c.)

Traveling priest
vanishing in mist,
trailed by his bell.

From the vast sky,
pulse
of starling wings.

Splat!
through the sluice-gate,
bellies of frogs.

Meisetsu (1847–1926)

Death at last—
little by little
fading of medicine odors.

Dakotsu (1885–1962)

My truths:
Buddha, green
ears of barley.

Winter evening—
shadow and I,
writing about me.

Snow falling
in and out
the water.

Seisensui (20th c.)

Song of the river
leads me
to my village.

To the end of time,
journeying,
cutting toe-nails.

Dragonfly
perched on my shoulder,
out for a stroll.

Tramping farther,
farther—
one green hill after another.

Santoka (1882–1940)

Beggar passes—
shadow to sunlight,
sunlight to shadow.

Shikunro (20th c.)

Frozen together
in one dream—
sea-slugs.

Even housebound
the winter fly
follows the sun.

Seisi (1869–1937)

Sudden shower
on my face—nine gallons
of lust rinsed off.

Koyo (1867–1903)

Winter storm—
at the stone wall
a drift of ducks.

All that God offers—
this path across
the parched moor.

Late spring rain—
again I must become
just me.

Hekigodo (1873–1937)

Ladybird takes off,
wings
parting her in two.

Water birds,
busy drawing lines
between themselves.

Suju (20th c.)

Town sky—
one new thing,
the swallows.

Suddenly
remembering her,
his feet crushed gravel.

Autumn sun—
dead friend's hand
warm on my shoulder.

Horse, carting
winter sunlight
on his back.

Kusatao (20th c.)

Mid-winter—crow
drops down
on its own shadow.

Fukio (1903–1930)

Sick of earth,
lark rises, singing,
from the heart.

Talking stops—
white petals
falling in my heart.

Takeo (20th c.)

Cricket chirp—
now
my life is clear.

Hakuu (1911–1936)

Kneeling
to a chrysanthemum—
how calm my life.

Shuoshi (20th c.)

Again, blood from
my lungs—how clear
my loved ones' faces.

Shikaku (20th c.)

Fallen leaves—
white hands of invalids
round the bonfire.

Crane carries
my passion
into the autumn night.

Left by
the firefly,
grass bends low.

Hakyo (1913–1969)

New grass—
gently, gently
I tread on clouds.

Horse—
up to its ears
in radishes.

Bosha (1900–1941)

My hair's falling fast—
this afternoon
I'm off to Asia Minor.

Shinkichi (1901–1987)

Autumn storm—
faces drawing close
in candle-light.

Sekito (20th c.)

Flame passing
from stick to stick—
such quiet.

My wife—
blurred in my right eye,
clear in my left.

Sojo (1901–1956)

Frog, so green—
are you
fresh painted?

Winter wind—
sardine's still
ocean-colored.

White chrysanthemums—
light/dark,
even their smell.

      Akutagawa (1892–1927)

I live with Buddha,
but when cold
I long for mortals.

Into the cage of
fireflies, mostly dead,
I send a breath.

      Kasho (20th c.)

Bird song—
a thin dust
on the piano.

      Hajime (20th c.)

Cricket—
with every chirp
the house grows older.

Dead thrush,
leaving me
to spread its wings.

Smelting furnace,
under the green
mountain of July.

Praying mantis
straddling a wasp—
how crisp each bite.

In this wasted field
here in my palm—
sunset.

Deepening my grief,
snap
of a branch.

Dewy night,
blazing stars—
I'll live forever.

Where has it flown,
snowcap
of Mount Ibuki?

Keeping snow at bay—
fence
of the Zen Hall.

I stopped—
the stream
flowed off alone.

Long have I
used it, body
damp with dew.

As long as I stand
on the cliff edge,
crabs stay put.

Seishi (20th c.)

Winter light
touches the Great Buddha,
then the hills.

Tatsuko (20th c.)

Reaching for the heart
of spring—
wind from tree to tree.

Aro (1879–1951)

A bit of sun—
world's full
of drying socks.

Ichirinso (20th c.)

Sea-slug, what kind
of Buddha
will you be?

Seisetsu (1871–1917)

Dying grasshopper,
grasping
a clod of earth.

Winter brook—
flowering on a pebble,
a sprig of water.

Spring rain—
could it be
the ghost of stones.

Kijo (1865–1938)

Over the mantis
I cup my hand—
a mantis.

Trees lost in haze—
a glint far off
becomes a heron.

Shuson (20th c.)

Coughing into
leafless trees—
the sky coughs back.

Dried reeds—
I cart them home,
in my eyes.

Kakio (1902–1962)

After hateful words,
I roar off
like a motorcycle.

Feels at home
here in the slums,
the butterfly.

Red smoke lifts
from the steel mill—
a tired arm.

Tota (20th c.)

New Poems (1997)

War Song

It was the moment summer
sounds breathless, drifts
into bittersweet autumn,

and the woody resonance
of poplars braced for winds
to come. And the tremor

of rushes sparked passion,
and mothers were laughing
and fathers aimed children

into the cloudless sky,
caught them giggling,
begging for more. Babies

blossomed, pulses of lovers
ticked over like restless
bees. Rumors came faster than

thoughts, and the news was war.

2

In the hush before
morning, amber of street
lamps, pinpricks of

stars, frantic dreams
slipped away, as light
swallowed darkness

through open windows
a desolate season of
chill air seeped in.

While fathers, sons,
lovers, spare kit in
duffles, marched down

the highroad, caught
in a maelstrom to
goodness knows where.

"Keep a stiff upper lip,"
they said, "back before
trees turn red." Lovers

were sighing, children were
whining, babies were fussing
because mothers were crying.

3

Leaves became draughts of
birds racing in bitter
wind, bare branches pointing

like fists clenched in grief.
But as the lull dawdled on,
weeks, months turned over,

and lovers wrote letters
till fingers were thumbs.
And mothers hummed once

again, kettles boiled shrilly,
babes suckled and burped
content as before. And

the children paraded, sticks
harnessed to shoulders.
They took sides and hated,

and took turns at killing,
then went home forgiven
because they were friends.

Columbines reared heads
in summer's kaleidoscope,
roses by hollyhocks scented

the day. The old with their
whispers of old wars
mulled over, while children

linked daisies and wore
them as crowns. Babes sleeping
in shade, smiled through cicada

chant. Mothers, lovers sought
news that would bring their
men home. It was then that

the warning came, rising
and falling, and bird song
was lost in the droning of

planes. Like comets of fire
and ice bombs were colliding.
Time splintered, walls

shattered, real war had come.
And as the smoke fizzled,
and fires were gutted, a hush

settled in. No mothers for
crying, no lovers for sighing,
no babies for fussing, no

children for whining.
            And
soon through the rubble
wild flowers were blooming.

Blank Page

What's to become
of it? Anything,
nothing? Could it

change the world?
Blot time from eyes,
ink through puddles

of pain, leaf by
the dead-letter office
of soul? Or race

over shadows of
Stinking Creek Road
by the Cumberland Gap

where fireflies lamp
a lone cat in a stand-
off with butterflies?

Could it change
with a comma, this
urge to fold over,

crease into a bird,
aim it soaring
through space forever?

Web

Stumped for words
I watch
the spider, nimble
vagabond,

shuttle among twigs
of the ever-

green. Its patience
    mesmerizes.

From my pen a thread
    crisscrosses
lines of silk into
    a geometric

sphere, a fragile cup,
    to filter
morning sun into
    my window,

frescoing the wall.

Doodle

Ink flows beyond the first
range of hills, endlessly
follows a silent path. Slips

by the clutter of cities,
skirting pure landscape, down
to the ocean. Out of a blot,

tangled in wind, come a plaintive
gull song, an urgent whale call
rumbling throughout the deep.

The last cry of victims, lost
in the pull of a restless tide
that draws down images of planets,

like frail moths ringing the stars.

The Search

The stranger fast
approaching, as I
fill my eyes with

wild flowers, would
think me odd, weird,
daft, were I to offer

him my secret. Could
I trust him,
would he understand

this need to fashion
images of cocksfoot,
couplets from the

evening primrose, wring
music from a thistle?
As he passes, lifts

his hand in greeting,
I tell him nothing,
not a word.

Woolgathering

Caught in a web of
sweat and ginger, I
review day's efforts,

my butterfingered
phrases choking the
rubbish bin. Dream

I'm the Roman poet
Cinna, threatened by
the mob for my bad verse.

Want to escape this
twanging of the nerves,
find clear as silk

a brushstroke in the
sun. Rewind the music,
take a giant leap, backwards.

Shrine of the Crane

(Yamaguchi, Japan)

Once, far back in time, moving
as slow shadows in a mime by
the stone lanterns, chipped,

discolored now, processions
of shrine maidens, vestal sprigs
crossed at their breasts, led

by stiff-robed priests, black
lacquered clogs tap-tapping on
the path, filed by worshippers

under red *toriis,* up the stone steps,
passing three fox shrines aflush
with offerings, coins, rice cakes,

twigs embroidered with a paper-twist
of prayer. Today those hungry
ghosts with lofty dreams have fled

the hum of useless prayer on prayer,
to get ahead, outstrip, outdo,
all dreams lost somewhere in the fold

of time, deaf to the song of cranes.

Visiting My Father

My father, who would take
his belt to me for telling
whoppers when I was a boy,
now whispers secrets on our

autumn walks. Daydreams
spill with leaves that
shimmy by us, freckling
the grass. Words leap from

the shadow of his 93-year
skirmish, become the bullet
searing through him on
the Western Front. Fame's

thrust upon him for his
sculpture of primeval man.
Cautiously I gesture where
geese fan over, ribboning

the sky. But lost in fancy
he unveils his monumental
visions in museums through
the world. Turning by remnants

of blue asters, chicory and
Queen Anne's lace, we hug
farewell. He stares into my
eyes, assuring me that dons

of Oxford, Moscow, the Sorbonne
call daily for his expertise.
Driving home, I pull up for
a field mouse, watch him dart

back into ripened corn. Passing
a stand of maple canopies,
I need to touch, hold onto,
run my fingers through their gold.

Black Bean Soup

I shadow the pond
patient as stone, catch
the sadness of wind
carving seashells

in traces of snow
in the park. Last
night, found my wife
sobbing at words in

her crossword puzzle.
There it was—
Black Bean Soup. And
there was my father,

months before dying,
asking in, out of
shadows for black
bean soup. My sister

and I watched him
leaving us slowly. My
thoughts back in time,
nearly seventy years,

tramping through snow,
hands clasped, off
to the park. "Snow,"
he said. "Snow," I said.

Laughing together, sliding
back home. Stamping
feet on the doormat,
eager for mother's good

soup, rich and thick.
Light and dark are memories,
like mountain junipers
snared by the kudzu,

ghosts for all time.
A tabby, half cocked
on a garden wall, shakes
off snowflakes, springs

down, rubs against me
like an old friend
as I pass. In spite of
death the winter cherry

blooms. A bird flies sharp
against the chill gray sky.

Waiting for the Light

They have laid down their
plowshares: mile upon mile
along Quentin Road villas

blossom on richest soil in
the U.S.A. New developments—
Goose Cove, Hunter's Creek,

Willow Bend—sprout where
the corn grew so high. Pulling
up as the light turns red

on the corner of Route 22,
by a woodframe house, man, woman
and boy are having it out on

the lawn. The man shakes his
fist, the woman reacts in kind,
the boy, hoarse with outrage,

runs insides, slamming the door.
As the light changes, I rev off
into what's left of the day.

On the Way to Rockford

On the scenic route down
Cherry Valley Road in a freak
blizzard, windshield wipers

stropping at the ice—squinting
at glazed branches doodling
the backdrop of the sky, I slow

down as I come upon the tipsied
farmhouse, county eyesore,
rubbish heap of skeletal barn,

sheds, car parts, rusted tractor,
pickup, now phantom sculptures
under snow. No sign of the old

man, who in summer basks with
dog, cat, chickens on his sinking
stoop, a lone philosopher. As

I pass by a cow stares upward
from the frozen patch, a curtain
in an upstairs window moves.

Reverie

Caught in the song
of playgrounds,
drifts of children's
voices coil like smoke.

I pass, yet cannot
leave these joyous
rousers. Glance back
over my shoulder,

remembering the hit
and run of time.

Spinning my son, my
daughter, then my

grandson, faster,
faster on the roundabout
near primrose banks
and bluebell woods,

where I, a child
among them, orbit
through trees chained
together by the sun.

April Showers

Sheer gray beauty, clouds
move in and out the day,
drive brushstrokes of rain
along the gutters, drenching

me, and the old wino guzzling
daily by the corner church,
chuckling to himself, foul-
mouthing passers by. Today

he starts out hunched over
a puddle, stirring rainbows
with his walking stick.
Uninvited witness, I clear

off before he ferrets out
my need to stir up colors of
the street—his boozy flush,
prisms of laburnum, almond,

cherry blossoms, misted bluebells,
iridescent songbirds. Rustling
the bold wash of spring
into a rainbow of my very own.

Student

Oddly, the lone sound
of the white stick
steers the blind girl
through the classroom

door. The look behind
her eyes, a poem-in-waiting.
Running her fingers over,
fine-tuning lines of

Yeats's "Second Coming,"
she stares into a void
strung out with stars.
And the miracle comes

as she reads out slowly,
softly, voice rising with
passion, music caught up
in the wind, leaving the room

in a silence richly dark.

And Still Birds Sing

1 Snapshots

Here we are together, clearing
out the past: old letters,
cuttings, photographs, crossing
our palm with memories, rich

as wildflowers, making room for
what will be, sum of our ups
and downs. Naked as shadows under
a waterfall of rose and silver

flashing between clouds, we stumble
in and out forgotten streets. Wonder:

Where's this? What's that? Fingering
images of loved ones, slipped by

sudden as a downburst, fleeter than
dancers waiting the last flute call.
Stare back over shoulders, as time
unraveling like silk leads us through

a path of broom, thrift and forget-
me-nots, where goodbys are forever.
Hold onto those we thought would
never leave, our children grown and gone.

Recall with belly-laughs the antics of
our son, our daughter and our grandson.
Within the filigree of borders follow
them to where their dreams have led.

Among the orange grass, cornflowers,
harebells, cowslips, ochre mountains
of our treks we stare in silence
at an irreplaceable light.

2 Newspaper Cuttings

Why did we keep these items, these
reports of World War II, these horror
stories of the living dead, eyes burning
through barbed wire? Still, those

tortured ones, men, women, children
moved from nightmare, kissed the hands
of liberators. Why did we save this
grim account of bodies of young soldiers

in Vietnam, piled high in an oxcart,
waiting the last lap of their journey
home? And still sun shone. We smooth
out headlines of a twister that wiped out

a town, rode trees and homes like thistledown
across the highway, left survivors

wandering in an alien place. Still, they
sifted rubble for the pieces that made up

their lives. We open up a page, stare
at the orphans in the ruins of Chechnya
huddled together, and the copy reads,
"They sing to calm the night." Nearby

a little girl points to a woman, face down
in the mud, says, "That's my mother.
Can you bury her?" Death offered up no
sound. And still birds sang. We feel

the need to leave this trail of pain, this
ravaging history. Take a rest from wounds
of deep reopened scars. Let poems tumbleweed
by cornfields turned to lakes in a new flood,

trees richened by rains, wildflowers run
a-riot from these flashfloods out of season.
Together, we ride by the periwinkle blue
of chicory, Queen Anne's lace, and yellow

asters in soft grasses, tiger lilies, goldenrod
and trumpet vines, clusters of sunflowers,
vetch and mustard, and we wonder at
the cruelty in such a lovely world.

3 Letters

Reading them, remembrance takes off
like clear paw prints in the snow.
Voices overwhelm us—a litany of
family and friends drawn as a thrum

of bees, nudging our hearts, muddling
with us through the ebb and flow of years,
searching the letter-box for fragments
we clung onto, like cockleburs, which

stirred up cravings for more news on
fragile paper, proof of our yesterdays.

We look into each other's eyes. We
cannot clear them out, will have to find

another corner for what's yet to come.
Replace them where we found them,
snapshots, cuttings, letters. Through the
open windows feel the season changing, once

again leaves turning in autumn, squirrels
gallivanting in the branches, and
the cat across the way crouched in the
bushes, set to pounce. And still birds sing.

Shopping

On our weekly jaunt into
the supermart my wife and I
part company among the green-
groceries—the martyr in me
takes his punishment without
a gripe. While she pokes
at bananas, veg, finecombs
a lettuce, chooses her iris,
daffodils, a bit of green,
I traipse along the aisles,
outflanking pushcarts, dodging
elbows, baskets. Steer by
baked beans, brooms, sultanas,
marmalade and nuts, All Bran,
pickled cabbage. Passing the
cat and dog food I'm confronted
by a man who seems to know me,
plasters me against the toilet
paper and begins the complex
story of his life. By now my
wife is going through the check-
out. I try to get a word in
while he's through with affair
number three and coming up to
four. I take my courage in my

hands, tell him I've got to go.
Take off, heave bags into our
old car's trunk as he comes up
behind me to conclude his tale.
Says, "What's your name again?"
Then, with a puzzled frown—
"Hey, do I know you?"

Meditation

Morning at my desk as the first
whirligig of light springs me
from my reverie—the canvas
of my mind fills with the brick

wall of the offices across
the way, windows phosphorescing,
and the face. Curtains parted,
eyes monitor my every smudge

that taps into those earphones,
scrambles the computer. I sit
here with my pen, aware we are
communicators in a fragile world

where ravaged towns and villages
glow red as berries on
the mountain ash, before the
daylight, swallowed, draws us close.

Pigeon in the Rain

On my morning jaunt
across Queen Mary's Garden
I wait in pelting rain
before a flash of pigeons

settles in my path.
Preening feathers, sorting
through the bushes,
unruffled by the absent

feeders bearing crumbs
in plastic bags. A
gallivanter puffs his
breast, vibrates in

courtship, scorned by
one, another. He's
content to turn tail
on the roses, flit

from branch to trellis,
drift through the
downpour toward clouds,
fly into my poem.

Colonel Mustard

I pass the old man cranking
up his record player on
the pavement, in all weathers,
tap-dancing on the spot,

faster in winter, slow in
this sultry heat. Head bent
under a frayed bowler, eyes
shifting, following the feet

skedaddling by—
"Any small change, please?"
Emptiness flows through the ink-
brush of ideas, fills spaces

in between clouds, and shoes
beating to a cranked-out tune.
And eyes insisting life's
a cock-up in a bleak and lonely

corner, where people do not
stop to mingle with the living
dead, but turn their faces
sharply from his stage. Since

pity's not enough, his taps
hurl spears into the crowds.
His drama fills their day—
"Any small change, please?"

London Matinée

Three strangers at the bus stop,
walk-ons in a farce, squint
into distance, lines best forgotten.

Road a blank script, no cue forthcoming:
posters, like backdrops, staging
an image. Framed in the shadows,

leading to nowhere, three strangers
at the bus stop, newspapers underarm—
promise of scenes to come: violence,

dreams gone sour, love-twists, freak
blizzards, wars in the distance. They
eye one another, marooned in a silence.

Delivery

Here he comes, the postman,
destiny in his sack: bill, ad,
bungled address, ritual of

acceptance or denial. The
tearing open on relief, on pain,
the send up of frustration

penciled in the dark museum
of the brain. Sit back on
my heels, watch his shadow

close in on the door. No wish
to confront him—blame
the messenger for all he drops

into my letter box, all he does not.

Airing New Shoes

My Sears 440
joggers on
the flagstones

by the hedge
reek of
formaldehyde,

send ant tribes
into exile
under violets

in the grass.
Birds hover,
will not light

near the offending
twosome that
will take me

rigged and sweaty
on my lick-split
round the park.

Bosnia

Trees still bend in the winds
of Bosnia, while the fool's-harvest
of death is tallied each day.

As the candle burns down, and the
ritual of living goes on, shops
open and close, mosques, churches

are filled. The pot simmers,
as if awaiting the footsteps of
children out playing in snow—

soon to become silent snow angels
caught in bitter games of their
fathers, where in a pitiless landscape

nobody wins and the rules are not fair.
And we watch as the generals carp and
the victims bleed on the ten o'clock news.

Docudrama

So many ways to suffer:
cast-offs, no-names, orphans
of Bogota run with rats,

lice-ridden dogs, scabied cats,
leery of the TV special
panning the great Cathedral,

trendy streets. They swarm from
hiding places, collar purses,
rip through cars, swiping their

daily bread from well-stocked
shelves. Merchants, swanky
shoppers, transfixed as a mural

drying on the wall, wait on the
death squad bullets to pick them
off like flies, bursting the bubble

of their bitter world. Blood,
a tear or so, shine on the stones,
frozen forever in a camera's eye.

The Round

Slowly, dark through
the sycamore shadows

the window, fuzzes wind-
dodging birds set down

in its branches. I listen
in wonder to icicles

chiming night rituals of
winter. Wait for dawn's

whirl-spin of light
and the shiver of wings.

For Helen, on Her Birthday

Somewhere, among wildflowers
        in a quiet place,
as yet undredged, untrampled,
        dearest,

is the small mound that one
        day will hold
a scrap of granite bearing
        our poor name.

When footsteps of our children,
        and their children
fade, do not despair. We will
        have begun

another journey into the unknown,
        content
as always, holding tightly
        to each other.

Voyage

That was the year midsummer's
heatwave knocked us all
for loops: cats, squirrels

up, down, round the oak and
sycamore, mobbed the birdbath,
scratched in frenzy at the camel-

back packed earth. Birds veered
cockeyed, whomped the kitchen
window. Grass snakes frizzled

on the concrete path. That
was the year mosquitoes
failed to guzzle, as I drifted

by the parched Kishwaukee River,
caught up with my wife
and daughter for a turn around

the park.
        Faltered as I
stepped down from the bridge.

2

That was the year the paramedics
strapped me in the helicopter,
pointed me to stars, in fits

and starts between the cockleburs
of galaxies, my eyes blurred up
with ghosts of mayhem, fireflies,

outcasts sifting garbage on hot
city streets. That was the year
on hold. Riddled with lifelines

in an alien bed, I thumbed the Sunday
bookpage, stared at faces of those
Auschwitz children waiting a turn

upon the Zyklon carrousel—near
the last photograph of Primo Levi,
their fire-eyed witness, before

he took his life,
                            slamming
the door on half a century's pain.

3

And this year, botched up
once again, oxygen mask in
place, heart monitor intact,

cut off from warzone static,
buzz and scuttle of the
misery out there. My wife,

my dearest friend, stroked
the blue flower round
the IV in my arm, coaxed

darkness from my eyes.
With tapestries of words
sent acrobatic sparrows

rising like last autumn's
leaves from fresh-turned soil,
wove flocks of scarlet tanagers

above gold-sovereign dandelions,
unthreaded winter hair of
willows greening into spring.

And this year, back full
circle in the summer heat,
I know for all it lacks

this world is still the only
place, and walking in a flame
of sunset I have things to do.

A Note about the Author

Lucien Stryk is a poet, translator, and essayist, and Distinguished Professor Emeritus of English at Northern Illinois University in DeKalb. In addition to writing, he is active as a lecturer.